THE BIBLE JESUS READ

Leader's Guide

Resources by Philip Yancey

The Jesus I Never Knew

What's So Amazing About Grace?

The Bible Jesus Read

Reaching for the Invisible God

Where Is God When It Hurts?

Disappointment with God

The Student Bible, General Edition (with Tim Stafford)

Meet the Bible (with Brenda Quinn)

Church: Why Bother?

Finding God in Unexpected Places

I Was Just Wondering

Soul Survivor

Books by Philip Yancey and Dr. Paul Brand

Fearfully and Wonderfully Made

In His Image

The Gift of Pain

PHILIP YANCEY

with

Stephen and Amanda Sorenson

THE BIBLE JESUS READ

Leader's Guide

An 8-Session Exploration of the Old Testament

GRAND RAPIDS, MICHIGAN 49530 USA

ZONDERVAN™

The Bible Jesus Read Leader's Guide

Requests for information should be addressed to:

Zondervan, *Grand Rapids, Michigan 49530*

ISBN: 0-310-24184-7

Interior design by Todd Sprague

Printed in the United States of America

04 05 06 07 08 09/❖ VG/ 10 9 8 7 6 5 4 3 2

CONTENTS

Preface

I have met many Christians who have only read the New Testament, not the Old. They may have tried to read the Old Testament here and there, but they found it too long, too disordered, or simply too strange. I sympathize, but at the same time I feel sad for those people because I don't think we get a full picture of how a life with God works from the New Testament alone.

The book I wrote, which we are studying here, is titled *The Bible Jesus Read* because, when you think about it, Jesus didn't have Paul's Epistles or the Gospels. So when he would go away and spend time meditating on God's Word, he used the Psalms, the Prophets, the books of Moses. That's where Jesus believed his relationship with God the Father was formed and examined.

When I meet people who tell me they were bored by or had a hard time reading the Old Testament, I say, "Welcome to the club!" It takes work. The Old Testament is a long book, and parts of it are slow. What I have found, though, is that the more work you put into it the more you'll get out of it. This Leader's Guide and accompanying materials in this Zondervan*Groupware*™ curriculum will give you a set of tools and approaches that will help you interpret the Old Testament and appropriate its wisdom.

I find it is helpful for me just to remember what the Old Testament is. The Old Testament is God's living message to us. It consists of truths he wants us to know about himself, about us, and about life.

The effort and commitment you put into your study of the Old Testament—including these Zondervan*Groupware* sessions—will yield a richness and value I believe you cannot obtain from any other source. This is, after all, the Bible Jesus read.

Philip Yancey

How to Use This Guide

This Leader's Guide is divided into eight sessions approximately 55 minutes in length. Each session corresponds to a videotaped presentation by Philip Yancey, and all but Session Two are based on individual chapters found in the book *The Bible Jesus Read*, published by Zondervan. The first two sessions present the Old Testament in broad strokes, while subsequent sessions focus on samplings of the people and major categories of Old Testament literature.

Although this guide can be used for individual study, it is designed primarily for group study. It can be used for retreats, in small group studies, or as a Sunday school elective.

BEFORE THE FIRST SESSION

- Make sure you have items mentioned below.
- Watch the videotaped presentation for this session.
- Obtain the necessary Participant's Guides for all participants.

For each session the *leader* will need:

- Leader's Guide
- Bible (Old and New Testaments)
- TV with video player (stand, extension cord, etc.)
- The course videotape
- Watch or clock with which to monitor time
- Extra pens or pencils if needed by participants

Note: For some sessions, you may also want to use an overhead projector, whiteboard, or flip chart.

For each session, the *participants* will need:

- Participant's Guide
- Bible (Old and New Testaments)
- Pen or pencil

KEY TYPOGRAPHICAL ELEMENTS

Directions for the Leader

Directions to the leader are shown in boxed, shaded areas. These directions are not meant to be read to the group.

Supplemental Materials

Various boxes and charts throughout the Leader's and Participant's Guides provide supplemental information that will enhance and deepen participants' understanding of the themes of the sessions. This material is not required reading to complete the session. If your group has more time available than the typical one-hour time slot, you may include the supplemental information as part of your session. Otherwise, these are available as additional resources for participants who want to deepen their study on their own.

Other boxes feature significant quotations that explain, supplement, and enhance the session. Many of these quotations would also be excellent discussion starters. Finally, throughout the sessions, key group-oriented questions for participants are followed by possible responses. These possible responses are included in the boxed leader's notes and will not only provide you with an inkling of the responses participants may give but will also guide you in emphasizing key points.

Corresponding Participant's Guide Pages

Session material is found on the left-hand pages of the Leader's Guide. On each facing right-hand page is a copy of the corresonding Participant's Guide page(s). There is also space on those right-hand pages for you to write in additional planning notes. Having the corresponding Participant's Guide page in front of you allows you to view the pages the participants are seeing as you talk without having to hold two books at the same time. It also lets you know where the participants are in their book when someone asks you a question.

HOW EACH SESSION IS DIVIDED

Each session is divided into six main parts: **Before You Lead, Introduction, Video Presentation, Group Discovery, Personal Journey,** and **Closing Meditation.** (Note: In Session 2, participants will not break into small groups, as they do in the other sessions.) A brief explanation of each part follows.

Before You Lead

Synopsis. Summarizes for the leader the material presented in each session.

Key Points of This Session. Highlights the key points on which the leader will want to focus.

Suggested Reading. Links each session to the related material in the book *The Bible Jesus Read* by Philip Yancey. (Note: Session 2 does not correspond to a specific chapter of *The Bible Jesus Read.*)

Session Outline. Provides an overview of the session's content, activities, and time frame.

Materials. A list of materials needed for the session.

Introduction

Welcome. Welcomes participants to the session.

What's to Come. A brief, introductory summary you may choose to use.

Questions to Think About. Designed to help everyone begin thinking about the theme(s) that will be covered. A corresponding page is included in the Participant's Guide.

Video Presentation

During this time, the leader and participants will watch the video and take notes. Key themes have been highlighted in both the Leader's and Participant's Guides.

Group Discovery

In this section, the leader will guide participants in thinking through key themes and information presented in each session. It is best to use the material in the order in which it is presented, but feel free to amplify various points with your own material or illustrations.

Video Highlights. Use these questions with the entire group. This will guide participants in verbally responding to key points and themes covered in the video. Some groups will discuss questions more freely and extensively than others. The questions are provided to keep discussion moving within less expressive groups. If you are leading an expressive group and find that you cannot complete as many questions as are provided, preselect key questions for your group to explore.

Large Group Exploration. During this time, you will guide the group in exploring a key theme or topic of the session. Often a few introductory sentences are provided that set the stage for discussion. Various approaches are used to stimulate learning and discussion. Sometimes questions are offered. Other times, participants will work together to complete charts or discuss Bible passages.

Small Group Exploration. At this time, if your group has more than seven participants you will break the group into small groups (three to five people). Participants will use their Bibles and write down suggested responses to the questions. If time allows, representatives of the small groups can share key ideas their groups discussed.

Group Discussion. Bring the entire group together to discuss additional questions that "wrap up" the session. As time allows, feel free to use the material as it is—or adapt it to the needs of your group.

Personal Journey

During this time, participants will have the opportunity to consider what they've discovered during the session and how it applies to their daily lives. Since this is a private, meditative exercise, participants should not talk among themselves. Participants also have the opportunity to continue their journey on their own by completing the To Do between Sessions portion.

Closing Meditation

You may close the session with the prayer provided, which has been adapted in part from a psalm. Or use a different prayer that fits the particular needs of your group.

TIPS ON LEADING AND PROMOTING GROUP DISCUSSION

1. Allow group members to participate at their own comfort levels. Everyone doesn't need to answer every question. It may take some participants a while to feel comfortable enough to share.
2. Ask questions with interest and warmth, then listen carefully to individual responses. Remember: it is important for participants to think through the questions and ideas presented as part of the process. The *process* is more important than specific answers, which is why possible responses are provided.
3. Be flexible. Reword questions if you wish. Choose to spend more or less time and add or delete questions to accommodate the needs of your group—and time frame.
4. Suggest that participants take time to explore any supplemental material that time did not permit them to explore within a session—and to review previous sessions. This review will be particularly helpful if each session is being done weekly, for example, rather than all eight sessions being done in a retreat setting.
5. Allow for (and expect) differences of opinion and experience.
6. Do not allow any person(s) to monopolize discussion. If such a situation arises, guide the discussion toward other people and perhaps speak to the person(s) afterward about the importance of allowing everyone to share.
7. If a heated discussion begins on a theological topic, suggest that participants involved continue their discussion with you after the session is over.

8. If you have time, read Philip Yancey's book *The Bible Jesus Read*, before or in conjunction with these sessions. Obviously not everything in his book could be included in these sessions. Reading the book will provide background that should help you in leading the discussions.
9. Monitor time frames without being heavy-handed. Although it's important to keep each session moving, remember that the needs of your group may cause you to spend more or less time on a particular part of a session. Also, keep in mind that the content of each session has been designed to enable participants to cover all of the intended material.
10. If time allows, invite participants to talk with you before or after the sessions about what they are learning and thinking. You can be an encouragement to them by listening, sharing ideas, sharing your experiences, etc.
11. Approach these sessions with a joyful heart. Many people have benefited from the opportunity to better understand the Old Testament and deepen their relationship with God as a result of *The Bible Jesus Read.*
12. Do not be afraid of silence. Allow people time to think—don't panic. Sometimes ten seconds of silence seems like an eternity. Remember, some of this material requires time to process—so give people time to digest a question and *then* respond.
13. Last, but certainly not least, ask people to pray for you and your group as you go through these sessions. God wants to do great things in your lives!

SESSION ONE

Is the Old Testament Worth the Effort?

BEFORE YOU LEAD

Synopsis

Knowledge of the thirty-nine Old Testament books–three-fourths of the Bible–is fading fast among Christians and has virtually vanished in popular culture. Many of us wonder, *Is the Old Testament worth the effort it takes to read and understand it?* We find ourselves asking such questions as:

- What is the point of studying about temples, priests, and rules for sacrifices that no longer exist? Some of that stuff is so boring!
- Why is the Old Testament so graphic? The violence in it offends me. I'm not sure I want my kids to read parts of it.
- Some portions of the Old Testament make no sense to me. Why, for example, did God care about defective sacrificial animals but apparently care little about pagan people like the Amalekites?
- I'm no history buff. Why should I care about ancient Middle-eastern customs, disputes, feuds, and marriages? What do those things have to do with me?
- How am I supposed to be able to make sense of the Old Testament and figure out how it applies to my life?
- Am I the only one who is confused by the Old Testament's mixed-up collection of poetry, history, sermons, and short stories written by so many different authors?

When he began reading the Old Testament, Philip Yancey identified with some of these same questions. Yet he was surprised to discover that the Old Testament satisfied a spiritual hunger in him that not even the New Testament could satisfy. "The Old Testament speaks to that hunger like no other book," he writes in *The Bible Jesus Read.* "It does not give us a lesson in theology, with abstract concepts neatly arranged in logical order. Quite the opposite: it gives an advanced course in Life with God, expressed in a style at once personal and passionate."

The people who appear in the Old Testament were real people learning to get along with the same God we worship. We can learn much from their experiences. By viewing the relationships between God and the Old Testament characters, we come to discover more about our own relationships with God.

Key Points of This Session

1. The Old Testament is a timeless, inspired message given to us by God that tells us what God wants us to know—about him, about life, and about ourselves.
2. The Old Testament gives us an advanced course in life with God and, in so doing, expands our concept of God and helps deepen our relationship with him.

Suggested Reading

This session corresponds to Chapter 1 of *The Bible Jesus Read.* You may want to read the Preface and Chapter 1 in order to deepen your understanding of this material.

Session Outline (54 minutes)

- I. Introduction (6 minutes)
  - A. Welcome
  - B. What's to Come
  - C. Questions to Think About
- II. Video Presentation: "Is the Old Testament Worth the Effort?" (11 minutes)
- III. Group Discovery (30 minutes)
  - A. Video Highlights (5 minutes)
  - B. Large Group Exploration: Why Read the Old Testament? (8 minutes)
  - C. Small Group Exploration: Opening the Curtain on a Bigger Picture of God (12 minutes)
  - D. Group Discussion (5 minutes)
- IV. Personal Journey (6 minutes)
- V. Closing Meditation (1 minute)

Materials

You'll need a VCR, TV, and Bible. You may also find a whiteboard, flip chart, or overhead projector to be useful in guiding group discussion. View the video prior to leading the session so that you are familiar with its main points.

SESSION ONE

Is the Old Testament Worth the Effort?

Apart from the Old Testament, we will always have an impoverished view of God. God is not a philosophical construct but a Person who acts in history: the one who created Adam, who gave a promise to Noah, who called Abraham and introduced himself by name to Moses, who deigned to live in a wilderness *tent* in order to live close to his people. From Genesis 1 onward, God has wanted himself to be known, and the Old Testament is our most complete revelation of what God is like.

—Philip Yancey

6 min. INTRODUCTION

Welcome

Welcome participants to Session 1 of The Bible Jesus Read course: "Is the Old Testament Worth the Effort?"

What's to Come

Knowledge of the thirty-nine Old Testament books—three-fourths of the Bible—is fading fast among Christians. Many of us wonder, *Is the Old Testament worth the effort it takes to read and understand it?*

As he began his venture into the Old Testament, author Philip Yancey asked the same question. When he delved into the Old Testament, he didn't uncover neatly ordered, abstract lessons in theology. Rather, he found himself involved in what he calls an advanced course in life with God—a course that was passionately presented through the lives of real people.

In this eight-session series, Philip Yancey will guide us in taking a fresh look at the Old Testament. We can learn so much from the people whose stories appear on its pages. They were real people learning to get along with the same God we worship. Their experiences and insights will help

NOTES

SESSION ONE

Is the Old Testament Worth the Effort?

> Apart from the Old Testament, we will always have an impoverished view of God. God is not a philosophical construct but a Person who acts in history: the one who created Adam, who gave a promise to Noah, who called Abraham and introduced himself by name to Moses, who deigned to live in a wilderness *tent* in order to live close to his people. From Genesis 1 onward, God has wanted himself to be known, and the Old Testament is our most complete revelation of what God is like.
>
> —Philip Yancey

Questions to Think About

1. When you hear the words "Old Testament," what thoughts and feelings come to mind?

2. What personal challenges have you faced when you have tried to read and understand the Old Testament?

3. What have you enjoyed about your ventures into the Old Testament, and what might be some of the benefits of becoming more familiar with it?

9

open up our understanding of what God is like and what it's like to be in a personal relationship with him.

Let's begin by considering a few questions. Please turn to page 9 of your Participant's Guide.

Questions to Think About

Participant's Guide page 9.

As time permits, ask two or more of the following questions and solicit responses from the participants.

1. When you hear the words "Old Testament," what thoughts and feelings come to mind?

Encourage participants to share honestly about their knowledge and views of the Old Testament. Encourage one-word responses, which may include: Psalms, scary, long, prophets, confusing, etc. Encourage longer answers as well, which may include: a series of books about people whose names are impossible to pronounce and who lived in places you can't even find on a map; a part of the Bible that has lots of violence; a collection of amazing stories like Daniel and the lions' den, Moses crossing the Red Sea, and David killing the giant Goliath; a hard-to-understand history book; a testimony of God's dealings with his people; etc.

2. What personal challenges have you faced when you have tried to read and understand the Old Testament?

Responses may include the fact that there are so many books, parts of it can be boring, it seems irrelevant, it's hard to relate to some of the ancient customs mentioned in the Old Testament, it's hard to know where to start reading, some books are complicated and hard to understand.

3. What have you enjoyed about your ventures into the Old Testament, and what might be some of the benefits of becoming more familiar with it?

Expect some diversity here. Be prepared to add some of your own ideas to stimulate discussion. Some individuals may believe that the Old Testament has little value. Others may mention such things as seeing the character of God unfold through various generations, learning more about what God is like, learning lessons from the heroes of the faith, gaining insights and wisdom from books like Proverbs, being able to read the Psalms when life is tough, etc.

Let's keep these ideas in mind as we view the video. There is space to take notes on page 10.

NOTES

SESSION ONE

Is the Old Testament Worth the Effort?

Apart from the Old Testament, we will always have an impoverished view of God. God is not a philosophical construct but a Person who acts in history: the one who created Adam, who gave a promise to Noah, who called Abraham and introduced himself by name to Moses, who deigned to live in a wilderness *tent* in order to live close to his people. From Genesis 1 onward, God has wanted himself to be known, and the Old Testament is our most complete revelation of what God is like.

—Philip Yancey

Questions to Think About

1. When you hear the words "Old Testament," what thoughts and feelings come to mind?

2. What personal challenges have you faced when you have tried to read and understand the Old Testament?

3. What have you enjoyed about your ventures into the Old Testament, and what might be some of the benefits of becoming more familiar with it?

9

11 min. VIDEO PRESENTATION: "IS THE OLD TESTAMENT WORTH THE EFFORT?"

Participant's Guide page 10.

Leader's Video Observations

God wants us to know about him

What Jesus read

Why read the Old Testament?

Discomfort is not bad

Honest feelings

30 min. GROUP DISCOVERY

If your group has seven or more members, use the Video Highlights with the entire group (5 minutes), then complete the Large Group Exploration (8 minutes), then break into small groups of three to five people for the Small Group Exploration (12 minutes). Finally, bring everyone together for the closing Group Discussion (5 minutes).

NOTES

Video Presentation: "Is the Old Testament Worth the Effort?"

God wants us to know about him

What Jesus read

Why read the Old Testament?

Discomfort is not bad

Honest feelings

If your group has fewer than seven members, begin with the Video Highlights (5 minutes), then complete both the Large Group Exploration (8 minutes) and the Small Group Exploration (12 minutes) as a group. Wrap up your discovery time with the Group Discussion (5 minutes).

Please turn to page 11 as we discuss some questions related to the video segment we have just seen.

Video Highlights (5 minutes)

Participant's Guide page 11.

As time permits, ask one or more of the following questions, which directly relate to the video the participants have just seen.

1. If the New Testament doesn't give a complete picture of what God wants us to know about him, what do you hope to learn from the Old Testament?

The Old Testament reveals more about God; is God's message to us; expands the history of our faith; gives insights into the history of the world; can help us with our problems; is realistic; helps us put words to our deepest emotions.

Refer participants to the box "Discovering the Old Testament" if your group needs additional ideas.

Discovering the Old Testament

There is so much of benefit for us to discover in the Old Testament. If only we would read it, we would:

- Gain a better understanding of the Old Testament concepts and allusions found in Hebrews, Jude, Revelation, and other New Testament books.
- Begin uncovering the layers of richness in the Epistles and Gospels that shed light backward on the Old Testament.
- Understand more about what God is really like and how he has worked—and is working—in the lives of his people.
- Benefit from the lessons of faith discovered by ancient Old Testament heroes.
- Have a richer, deeper understanding of the redemptive love story between God and his people that continues to unfold today.
- Begin to grasp the degree to which what we say, how we behave, and even what we think and feel influences God and how much he delights in us.
- Learn the lessons of faith—faith that is entirely human, yet rock-solid—that sustained so many Old Testament characters and can sustain us when we face life's challenges.

NOTES

Video Highlights

1. If the New Testament doesn't give a complete picture of what God wants us to know about him, what do you hope to learn from the Old Testament?

Discovering the Old Testament

There is so much of benefit for us to discover in the Old Testament. If only we would read it, we would:

- Gain a better understanding of the Old Testament concepts and allusions found in Hebrews, Jude, Revelation, and other New Testament books.
- Begin uncovering the layers of richness in the Epistles and Gospels that shed light backward on the Old Testament.
- Understand more about what God is really like and how he has worked—and is working—in the lives of his people.
- Benefit from the lessons of faith discovered by ancient Old Testament heroes.
- Have a richer, deeper understanding of the redemptive love story between God and his people that continues to unfold today.
- Begin to grasp the degree to which what we say, how we behave, and even what we think and feel influences God and how much he delights in us.
- Learn the lessons of faith—faith that is entirely human, yet rock-solid—that sustained so many Old Testament characters and can sustain us when we face life's challenges.

2. Which thoughts and emotions began to surface as you watched this video? What surprised you or stood out above the rest?

The key here is to encourage participants to share of themselves and start considering the journey into exploring the Old Testament. Points shared may include: feeling challenged to start thinking about some of the issues mentioned, wondering why the Old Testament is ignored by so many people, wishing that it were possible to go back in time and read the Old Testament sooner, etc.

3. Philip Yancey spoke of the relevance and realism of the Old Testament. What hope does the graphic realism of the Old Testament offer you in relationship to your walk with God?

Responses will vary. The most important thing is to encourage participants to begin thinking about the Old Testament and the personal, relevant message it holds for them.

Now we're ready for the Large Group Exploration part of this session. Please turn to page 13.

Large Group Exploration: Why Read the Old Testament? (8 minutes)

Participant's Guide page 13.

Read the introductory paragraph to the group, then begin discussing the questions that follow.

Years ago most people knew at least something about the Old Testament—the story of David and Goliath, some of the Ten Commandments, or the story of Noah. Today, however, knowledge of the Old Testament is fading fast among Christians and has virtually vanished in popular culture. Let's consider some of the challenges to and benefits of reading the Old Testament.

Perspective

The Old Testament is not, as one theologian suggested, "reading someone else's mail"; it is our mail as well. The people who appear in it were real people learning to get along with the same God that I worship. I need to learn from their experience even as I try to incorporate the marvelous new message brought by Jesus.

—Philip Yancey

NOTES

2. Which thoughts and emotions began to surface as you watched this video? What surprised you or stood out above the rest?

3. Philip Yancey spoke of the relevance and realism of the Old Testament. What hope does the graphic realism of the Old Testament offer you in relationship to your walk with God?

Large Group Exploration: Why Read the Old Testament?

Years ago most people knew at least something about the Old Testament—the story of David and Goliath, some of the Ten Commandments, or the story of Noah. Today, however, knowledge of the Old Testament is fading fast among Christians and has virtually vanished in popular culture. Let's consider some of the challenges to and benefits of reading the Old Testament.

Perspective

The Old Testament is not, as one theologian suggested, "reading someone else's mail"; it is our mail as well. The people who appear in it were real people learning to get along with the same God that I worship. I need to learn from their experience even as I try to incorporate the marvelous new message brought by Jesus.

—Philip Yancey

1. It's easy to think that we *ought* to read the Old Testament and therefore lump it into the same category as other things we *should* do—floss our teeth, exercise regularly, eat right, or listen more attentively to a spouse. In what ways have you felt obligated to read the Old Testament? If you have ever attempted to read through the Bible, such as in a "Read the Bible in a Year" program, how did it work out?

1. It's easy to think that we *ought* to read the Old Testament and therefore lump it into the same category as other things we *should* do—floss our teeth, exercise regularly, eat right, or listen more attentively to a spouse. In what ways have you felt obligated to read the Old Testament? If you have ever attempted to read through the Bible, such as in a "Read the Bible in a Year" program, how did it work out?

Encourage participants to evaluate why they approach the Old Testament the way they do. Responses will vary greatly. Some participants will barely have read it at all, some will have dabbled here and there in a seemingly futile search for meaning, and some will have intentionally avoided it. Still others may have started reading it out of a sense of obligation but have grown to love it.

2. From the reading or study you have done, describe the ways in which you have found the God featured in the Old Testament to be similar to or different from the God featured in the New Testament.

Responses will vary but may include that God desires to be in relationship with us and wants us to obey him in both Old and New Testaments; the God of the Old Testament speaks out much more about sin and dishes out huge penalties for it; the God of the Old Testament seems to focus almost exclusively on the Jews; the God of the New Testament is both powerful and full of glory (Revelation) yet appears as an all-too-human servant (Jesus); the Old Testament emphasizes more about God the Creator and keeper of the universe who is involved in its day-to-day workings; the Old Testament reveals more about how God works—slowly, unpredictably, paradoxically; it's easier to understand what God is doing, what his plan is, in the New Testament; etc.

3. As he walked along the road to Emmaus, Jesus explained to two of his grieving disciples "what was said in all the Scriptures concerning himself" (Luke 24:27). What does this tell us about Jesus' view of the Old Testament Scriptures? What does it reveal about his love for, commitment to, and understanding of the Old Testament?

Jesus loved the Scriptures and knew them well. He treasured them. He used them to communicate God's message. If time permits, you may give an example or ask participants to look up some of the instances when Jesus quoted the Scriptures. You will find that Jesus used the Old Testament Scriptures in his teaching ministry and in his confrontations with religious leaders who knew the Law, but not the heart, of the Scriptures. Jesus also quoted from the Scriptures in his encounter with Satan in the wilderness.

NOTES

Large Group Exploration: Why Read the Old Testament?

Years ago most people knew at least something about the Old Testament—the story of David and Goliath, some of the Ten Commandments, or the story of Noah. Today, however, knowledge of the Old Testament is fading fast among Christians and has virtually vanished in popular culture. Let's consider some of the challenges to and benefits of reading the Old Testament.

Perspective

The Old Testament is not, as one theologian suggested, "reading someone else's mail"; it is our mail as well. The people who appear in it were real people learning to get along with the same God that I worship. I need to learn from their experience even as I try to incorporate the marvelous new message brought by Jesus.

—Philip Yancey

1. It's easy to think that we *ought* to read the Old Testament and therefore lump it into the same category as other things we *should* do—floss our teeth, exercise regularly, eat right, or listen more attentively to a spouse. In what ways have you felt obligated to read the Old Testament? If you have ever attempted to read through the Bible, such as in a "Read the Bible in a Year" program, how did it work out?

2. From the reading or study you have done, describe the ways in which you have found the God featured in the Old Testament to be similar to or different from the God featured in the New Testament.

3. As he walked along the road to Emmaus, Jesus explained to two of his grieving disciples "what was said in all the Scriptures concerning himself" (Luke 24:27). What does this tell us about Jesus' view of the Old Testament Scriptures? What does it reveal about his love for, commitment to, and understanding of the Old Testament?

4. What unique perspectives on our relationship with God—including our doubts, struggles, and pain—might the Old Testament provide?

4. What unique perspectives on our relationship with God—including our doubts, struggles, and pain—might the Old Testament provide?

Without the perspective God reveals in the Old Testament, we miss some of the fullness of what God is like; we do not have the opportunity to see how "heroes" of the faith such as Moses and David grew in their relationship with God—how they blew it yet learned difficult lessons and continued to grow in their relationship with God; we miss understanding more about God's passionate love for his people and his desire to be in relationship with us; we miss out on the perspective of God working out his plan through centuries of history; etc.

Jesus Knew His Bible Well

Jesus often referred to the Old Testament writings and pointed out important facts about himself and his mission. The following chart reveals some of the times when Jesus quoted directly from the Old Testament.

Situation	What Jesus Said
Matthew 13:13–15; Mark 4:12	Isaiah 6:9–10
Mark 7:6–7	Isaiah 29:13
Mark 7:10	Exodus 20:12; 21:17; Leviticus 20:9; Deuteronomy 5:16
Mark 9:48	Isaiah 66:24
Mark 11:17	Isaiah 56:7
Luke 4:4	Deuteronomy 8:3
Luke 4:8	Deuteronomy 6:13
Luke 4:10–11	Psalm 91:11–12
Luke 4:12	Deuteronomy 6:16
Luke 4:18–19	Isaiah 61:1–2
Luke 7:27	Malachi 3:1
Luke 10:27	Deuteronomy 6:5
Luke 18:20	Exodus 20:12–16; Deuteronomy 5:16–20
Luke 20:17	Psalm 118:22
John 6:31	Exodus 16:4; Nehemiah 9:15
John 13:18	Psalm 41:9

Please turn to page 16 as we move into the Small Group Exploration part of this session.

NOTES

2. From the reading or study you have done, describe the ways in which you have found the God featured in the Old Testament to be similar to or different from the God featured in the New Testament.

3. As he walked along the road to Emmaus, Jesus explained to two of his grieving disciples "what was said in all the Scriptures concerning himself" (Luke 24:27). What does this tell us about Jesus' view of the Old Testament Scriptures? What does it reveal about his love for, commitment to, and understanding of the Old Testament?

4. What unique perspectives on our relationship with God—including our doubts, struggles, and pain—might the Old Testament provide?

Jesus Knew His Bible Well

Jesus often referred to the Old Testament writings and pointed out important facts about himself and his mission. The following chart reveals some of the times when Jesus quoted directly from the Old Testament.

Situation	What Jesus Said
Matthew 13:13–15; Mark 4:12	Isaiah 6:9–10
Mark 7:6–7	Isaiah 29:13
Mark 7:10	Exodus 20:12; 21:17; Leviticus 20:9; Deuteronomy 5:16
Mark 9:48	Isaiah 66:24
Mark 11:17	Isaiah 56:7
Luke 4:4	Deuteronomy 8:3
Luke 4:8	Deuteronomy 6:13
Luke 4:10–11	Psalm 91:11–12
Luke 4:12	Deuteronomy 6:16
Luke 4:18–19	Isaiah 61:1–2
Luke 7:27	Malachi 3:1
Luke 10:27	Deuteronomy 6:5
Luke 18:20	Exodus 20:12–16; Deuteronomy 5:16–20
Luke 20:17	Psalm 118:22
John 6:31	Exodus 16:4; Nehemiah 9:15
John 13:18	Psalm 41:9

Small Group Exploration: Opening the Curtain on a Bigger Picture of God (12 minutes)

Participant's Guide page 16.

To ensure that all questions are covered within your available time frame, you may want to assign specific questions to each group, then bring the groups together to share their discoveries.

The Old Testament reveals a rich picture of what God–the personal God who loves us and wants to be in relationship with us–is like. Let's break into groups of three to five and look at a few "snapshots" of what the Old Testament reveals about God and his relationship with us.

If you will not be breaking into small groups for the Small Group Exploration, lead the group in a discussion of the following questions.

1. What imagery did David use to describe God's care for his people? In what ways is this like or unlike the New Testament image of God? (See Psalms 17:8–9; 57:1; 91:1–4.)

David described God as sheltering his people under his wings, which is a very personal, very caring image. For some participants, a New Testament image of God may be more intellectual and less personal—more of the redeemer and ultimate judge of the human race, for example.

2. What does Isaiah 62:2–5 reveal about God's desire and love for his people? To what does he compare his relationship to his people? What is your response to these expressions of honor and delight?

God compares his relationship with us to a bridegroom rejoicing over his bride. In fact, he says that he rejoices over his people! This is significant today, when many people feel as if God doesn't really care about them or even believe that he is impersonal.

3. What imagery is used in Isaiah 40:9–11 to show God's love for his people?

God—the sovereign Lord of the universe—loves us. This is fantastic news! He tends us with loving care, as a shepherd cares for his sheep. Think of the shepherd holding a lamb close to his heart—that's how God feels about and cares for each of us.

4. The Old Testament records times when God allowed people to exert an influence on him as well as times when he exerted his influence on them. Discuss what happened in the following situations, particularly in terms of the relationship between God and his people.

   a. Genesis 18:22–33

Abraham negotiated with God about the future of Sodom, where Abraham's nephew, Lot, lived with his family. Their conversation is quite revealing—a respectful, bold, intimate interchange.

NOTES

Small Group Exploration: Opening the Curtain on a Bigger Picture of God

The Old Testament reveals a rich picture of what God—the personal God who loves us and wants to be in relationship with us—is like. Let's break into groups of three to five and look at a few "snapshots" of what the Old Testament reveals about God and his relationship with us.

1. What imagery did David use to describe God's care for his people? In what ways is this like or unlike the New Testament image of God? (See Psalm 17:8–9; 57:1; 91:1–4.)

2. What does Isaiah 62:2–5 reveal about God's desire and love for his people? To what does he compare his relationship to his people? What is your response to these expressions of honor and delight?

3. What imagery is used in Isaiah 40:9–11 to show God's love for his people?

4. The Old Testament records times when God allowed people to exert an influence on him as well as times when he exerted his influence on them. Discuss what happened in the following situations, particularly in terms of the relationship between God and his people.
   a. Genesis 18:22–33
   b. 1 Samuel 7:2–10

5. God wanted the ancient Hebrews to continually remind themselves that the world revolved around God, not themselves. Look up the following verses and describe what God commanded the Israelites to do in order to stay focused on him.
   a. Exodus 13:1–16
   b. Numbers 15:37–41

Perspective

I've met a lot of Christians who have only read the New Testament. They may have tried the Old Testament here or there, and found it a little off-putting and just gave up. I feel sad for those Christians, frankly, because I don't think we get a full picture of how a life with God works from the New Testament.

—Philip Yancey

b. 1 Samuel 7:2–10

The Israelites, who had been worshiping false gods, destroyed their idols and decided to serve only God. Then Samuel the prophet called out to God on Israel's behalf because they wanted to be freed from the Philistines' tyranny and saved from military defeat. God answered with such a loud thunder that the fearsome Philistine troops ran away in a panic. This story shows the dynamic, two-way nature of God's relationship with his people.

5. God wanted the ancient Hebrews to continually remind themselves that the world revolved around God, not themselves. Look up the following verses and describe what God commanded the Israelites to do in order to stay focused on him.

   a. Exodus 13:1–16

The Israelites were to dedicate every firstborn male—man or animal—to God. Every year, they were to celebrate the Feast of Unleavened Bread to commemorate the time when God delivered them from Egyptian bondage. These activities were to be ongoing reminders of their relationship with God.

   b. Numbers 15:37–41

The Israelites were to place tassels on the corners of their clothing to remind them to obey God's commands rather than to follow their own fleshly desires. God did this because, as he expressed it, "I am the Lord your God." This is a statement of close, essential relationship.

Perspective

> I've met a lot of Christians who have only read the New Testament. They may have tried the Old Testament here or there, and found it a little off-putting and just gave up. I feel sad for those Christians, frankly, because I don't think we get a full picture of how a life with God works from the New Testament.
>
> —Philip Yancey

If you have divided into small groups, let participants know when there is 1 minute remaining.

Give participants a moment to transition from their small group discussions. If time allows, or if you have assigned each group a specific question, have representatives from the groups share their key ideas.

Now let's wrap up our Group Discovery time. Please turn to page 18.

NOTES

4. The Old Testament records times when God allowed people to exert an influence on him as well as times when he exerted his influence on them. Discuss what happened in the following situations, particularly in terms of the relationship between God and his people.
   a. Genesis 18:22–33
   b. 1 Samuel 7:2–10
5. God wanted the ancient Hebrews to continually remind themselves that the world revolved around God, not themselves. Look up the following verses and describe what God commanded the Israelites to do in order to stay focused on him.
   a. Exodus 13:1–16
   b. Numbers 15:37–41

Perspective

I've met a lot of Christians who have only read the New Testament. They may have tried the Old Testament here or there, and found it a little off-putting and just gave up. I feel sad for those Christians, frankly, because I don't think we get a full picture of how a life with God works from the New Testament.

—Philip Yancey

Group Discussion (5 minutes)

Participant's Guide page 18.

Use one or more of the following questions to encourage participants to share their observations with the entire group.

1. The Old Testament is a timeless, inspired message given to us by God that tells us what God wants us to know–about him, about life, and about ourselves. In what ways has what we have seen and discussed together today influenced your view of the Old Testament?
2. The Old Testament gives us an advanced course in life with God and, in so doing, expands our concept of God and helps deepen our relationship with him. Take a few minutes to consider your personal relationship with God in light of what you have explored today.

Now it's time for each of us to consider on a personal level what we've been discussing and thinking about. Please turn to page 19.

6 min. PERSONAL JOURNEY: TO BEGIN NOW

Participant's Guide page 19.

No wonder those of us who have grown up with abstract concepts of God find it confusing to try to make logical sense out of the Old Testament! The Old Testament presents laws and history, but it also speaks to us in images of a God and Creator who desires to be in close relationship with us.

Take some time now by yourself to consider what you have discovered in this session and how it applies to your daily life.

Read Deuteronomy 6:1–12.

1. What kind of a relationship does this passage indicate God wants to have with his people?
2. What was God's overarching concern about his relationship with his people? What things did God want his people to do in order to preserve their relationship with him?
3. Jesus considered the command to "love the Lord your God with all your heart and with all your soul and with all your strength" to be the essential commandment. What can you incorporate into your daily life that will help you obey this commandment?

NOTES

Group Discussion

1. The Old Testament is a timeless, inspired message given to us by God that tells us what God wants us to know—about him, about life, and about ourselves. In what ways has what we have seen and discussed together today influenced your view of the Old Testament?

2. The Old Testament gives us an advanced course in life with God and, in so doing, expands our concept of God and helps deepen our relationship with him. Take a few minutes to consider your personal relationship with God in light of what you have explored today.

Personal Journey: To Begin Now

No wonder those of us who have grown up with abstract concepts of God find it confusing to try to make logical sense out of the Old Testament! The Old Testament presents laws and history, but it also speaks to us in images of a God and Creator who desires to be in close relationship with us.

Take some time now by yourself to consider what you have discovered in this session and how it applies to your daily life.

Read Deuteronomy 6:1–12.

1. What kind of a relationship does this passage indicate God wants to have with his people?

2. What was God's overarching concern about his relationship with his people? What things did God want his people to do in order to preserve their relationship with him?

3. Jesus considered the command to "love the Lord your God with all your heart and with all your soul and with all your strength" to be the essential commandment. What can you incorporate into your daily life that will help you obey this commandment?

Did You Know?

Unlike many Christians today, the New Testament Christians eagerly pursued the Old Testament Scriptures. They found in the Old Testament a wealth of understanding about the kind of relationship God desired to have with them. Paul, for example, constantly referred to the Old Testament in his writings. Note the many Old Testament connections that appear in the third chapter of Galatians alone!

Galatians 3	Old Testament Connections
v. 6 Mentions Abraham's belief	Genesis 15:6
v. 8 Mentions God's promise to bless all nations through Abraham	Genesis 12:3; 18:18; 22:18
v. 10 Quotes from the Old Testament Law	Deuteronomy 27:26
v. 11 Quotes from an Old Testament prophet	Habbakuk 2:4
v. 12 References the Old Testament Law	Leviticus 18:5
v. 13 Quotes an Old Testament verse	Deuteronomy 21:23
v. 16 Analyzes several Old Testament references	Genesis 12:7; 13:15; and 24:7

Did You Know?

Unlike many Christians today, the New Testament Christians eagerly pursued the Old Testament Scriptures. They found in the Old Testament a wealth of understanding about the kind of relationship God desired to have with them. Paul, for example, constantly referred to the Old Testament in his writings. Note the many Old Testament connections that appear in the third chapter of Galatians alone!

Galatians 3		Old Testament Connections
v. 6	Mentions Abraham's belief	Genesis 15:6
v. 8	Mentions God's promise to bless all nations through Abraham	Genesis 12:3; 18:18; 22:18
v. 10	Quotes from the Old Testament Law	Deuteronomy 27:26
v. 11	Quotes from an Old Testament prophet	Habbakuk 2:4
v. 12	References the Old Testament Law	Leviticus 18:5
v. 13	Quotes an Old Testament verse	Deuteronomy 21:23
v. 16	Analyzes several Old Testament references	Genesis 12:7; 13:15; and 24:7

Let participants know when there is 1 minute remaining. After 6 minutes have passed, remind participants that they may want to continue their journey by completing the additional exercise on page 21 of their Participant's Guide before the next session.

PERSONAL JOURNEY: TO DO BETWEEN SESSIONS

Before the next session, set aside at least one hour away from distractions to do the following exercise.

1. Take an inventory of what you believe about the Old Testament. List your likes and dislikes, the things that confuse or excite you, your favorite passages, etc. Be sure to include at least two ways in which you might benefit from further exploration of the Old Testament.
2. Write down some ways in which you might be able to use the above "inventory" to chart a new approach toward the Old Testament. For

NOTES

3. Jesus considered the command to "love the Lord your God with all your heart and with all your soul and with all your strength" to be the essential commandment. What can you incorporate into your daily life that will help you obey this commandment?

Did You Know?

Unlike many Christians today, the New Testament Christians eagerly pursued the Old Testament Scriptures. They found in the Old Testament a wealth of understanding about the kind of relationship God desired to have with them. Paul, for example, constantly referred to the Old Testament in his writings. Note the many Old Testament connections that appear in the third chapter of Galatians alone!

Galatians 3	Old Testament Connections
v. 6 Mentions Abraham's belief	Genesis 15:6
v. 8 Mentions God's promise to bless all nations through Abraham	Genesis 12:3; 18:18; 22:18
v. 10 Quotes from the Old Testament Law	Deuteronomy 27:26
v. 11 Quotes from an Old Testament prophet	Habbakuk 2:4
v. 12 References the Old Testament Law	Leviticus 18:5
v. 13 Quotes an Old Testament verse	Deuteronomy 21:23
v. 16 Analyzes several Old Testament references	Genesis 12:7; 13:15; and 24:7

Personal Journey: To Do between Sessions

Set aside at least one hour away from distractions to do the following exercise.

1. Take an inventory of what you believe about the Old Testament. List your likes and dislikes, the things that confuse or excite you, your favorite passages, etc. Be sure to include at least two ways in which you might benefit from further exploration of the Old Testament.

2. Write down some ways in which you might be able to use the above "inventory" to chart a new approach toward the Old Testament. For example, if you tend to be bored by all the history in the Bible, you may want to reread portions of it through the lens of a specific perspective. Instead of focusing on the violence or trying to follow the historic sequence, you may want to look for insight into God's character or look for evidence of his desire for relationship.

Perspective

It may prove dangerous to get involved with the Bible. You approach it with a series of questions, and as you enter it you find the questions turned back upon you. King David got swept up in a story by the prophet Nathan and leaped to his feet indignant—only to learn the barbed story concerned himself. I find something similar at work again and again as I read the Old Testament. I am thrown back on what I truly believe. I am forced to reexamine. . . . After spending time exploring the Old Testament, I can truthfully say that I come away more astonished, not less.

—Philip Yancey

example, if you tend to be bored by all the history in the Bible, you may want to reread portions of it through the lens of a specific perspective. Instead of focusing on the violence or trying to follow the historic sequence, you may want to look for insight into God's character or look for evidence of his desire for relationship.

Perspective

It may prove dangerous to get involved with the Bible. You approach it with a series of questions, and as you enter it you find the questions turned back upon you. King David got swept up in a story by the prophet Nathan and leaped to his feet indignant—only to learn the barbed story concerned himself. I find something similar at work again and again as I read the Old Testament. I am thrown back on what I truly believe. I am forced to reexamine. . . . After spending time exploring the Old Testament, I can truthfully say that I come away more astonished, not less.

—Philip Yancey

3. Begin reading the Old Testament. Consider how much of an investment you want to make in exploring the Old Testament and set a goal for yourself. If you get bogged down in a difficult area, feel free to take a refreshing break by going to one of your favorite Old Testament passages then approaching the more difficult passage again later, or, choose a new passage.

Two-Week Old Testament Reading Plan

The Student Bible has a two-week Old Testament reading plan that provides an overview of Old Testament highlights. If you are just beginning to study the Old Testament, it's a good way to start.

Day 1: Genesis 1—The story of Creation
Day 2: Genesis 3—The origin of sin
Day 3: Genesis 22—Abraham and Isaac
Day 4: Exodus 3—Moses' encounter with God
Day 5: Exodus 20—The gift of the Ten Commandments
Day 6: 1 Samuel 13—David and Goliath
Day 7: 2 Samuel 11—David and Bathsheba
Day 8: 2 Samuel 12—Nathan's rebuke of the king
Day 9: 1 Kings 18—Elijah and the prophets of Baal
Day 10: Job 38—God's answer to Job
Day 11: Psalm 51—A classic confession
Day 12: Isaiah 40—Words of comfort from God
Day 13: Daniel 6—Daniel and the lions
Day 14: Amos 4—A prophet's stern warning

NOTES

Personal Journey: To Do between Sessions

Set aside at least one hour away from distractions to do the following exercise.

1. Take an inventory of what you believe about the Old Testament. List your likes and dislikes, the things that confuse or excite you, your favorite passages, etc. Be sure to include at least two ways in which you might benefit from further exploration of the Old Testament.

2. Write down some ways in which you might be able to use the above "inventory" to chart a new approach toward the Old Testament. For example, if you tend to be bored by all the history in the Bible, you may want to reread portions of it through the lens of a specific perspective. Instead of focusing on the violence or trying to follow the historic sequence, you may want to look for insight into God's character or look for evidence of his desire for relationship.

Perspective

It may prove dangerous to get involved with the Bible. You approach it with a series of questions, and as you enter it you find the questions turned back upon you. King David got swept up in a story by the prophet Nathan and leaped to his feet indignant—only to learn the barbed story concerned himself. I find something similar at work again and again as I read the Old Testament. I am thrown back on what I truly believe. I am forced to reexamine. . . . After spending time exploring the Old Testament, I can truthfully say that I come away more astonished, not less.

—Philip Yancey

3. Begin reading the Old Testament. Consider how much of an investment you want to make in exploring the Old Testament and set a goal for yourself. If you get bogged down in a difficult area, feel free to take a refreshing break by going to one of your favorite Old Testament passages then approaching the more difficult passage again later, or, choose a new passage.

Two-Week Old Testament Reading Plan

The Student Bible has a two-week Old Testament reading plan that provides an overview of Old Testament highlights. If you are just beginning to study the Old Testament, it's a good way to start.

Day 1: Genesis 1—The story of Creation
Day 2: Genesis 3—The origin of sin
Day 3: Genesis 22—Abraham and Isaac
Day 4: Exodus 3—Moses' encounter with God
Day 5: Exodus 20—The gift of the Ten Commandments
Day 6: 1 Samuel 13—David and Goliath
Day 7: 2 Samuel 11—David and Bathsheba
Day 8: 2 Samuel 12—Nathan's rebuke of the king
Day 9: 1 Kings 18—Elijah and the prophets of Baal
Day 10: Job 38—God's answer to Job
Day 11: Psalm 51—A classic confession
Day 12: Isaiah 40—Words of comfort from God
Day 13: Daniel 6—Daniel and the lions
Day 14: Amos 4—A prophet's stern warning

1 min. CLOSING MEDITATION

Let's take a moment to close in prayer.

Dear God, thank you for the opportunity to begin learning more about the Old Testament and discovering more about you. In many ways we are exploring new territory. We're asking new questions about the Bible, and we need your guidance and wisdom. Thank you for loving each of us, for wanting to be in relationship with us no matter who we are or what we've done. Please guide us in the sessions to come. There is so much waiting for us in the Bible Jesus read, and we want to be receptive to what you want to say to us. In your name we pray, amen.

—Prayer inspired by Psalm 100

NOTES

SESSION TWO

Understanding the Old Testament

BEFORE YOU LEAD

Synopsis

The Old Testament is full of things God wants us to know—about himself, about ourselves, and about life. Although it has thousands of pages, dozens of heroes and villains, and was written over a span of at least five hundred years, the Old Testament tells a single, coherent story. This session highlights that story, providing a context through which we can begin to understand the Old Testament.

The video for this session provides participants with a "broad sweep" of the Old Testament story, which Philip summarizes in just a few words: "God creates a world and a family. He loses that family, and then he gets it back."

The story opens with creation—two people in Paradise—but things soon go downhill. Before long, God laments that he made human beings at all. But God does not give up. He comes up with a new plan to show his love to the human race. He chooses Abraham and promises to create from his offspring a great nation through which God will declare his message to the world.

During what's called the Patriarchal Age, Abraham and his wife, Sarah, have a son named Isaac, who in turn has a son named Jacob whom God later renames Israel. Jacob's twelve sons establish the twelve tribes of Israel from which the rest of the Old Testament story flows. But the unfolding story isn't a smooth one. Joseph, one of Jacob's sons, is sold by his brothers as a slave. God uses this incident to save Jacob's family (and the future nation of Israel) from a famine, but it leads to hundreds of years of slavery in Egypt.

God then raises up Moses to lead the twelve tribes out of Egypt (the Exodus). Over time, with God's help, the Israelites build an empire that seems destined to fulfill God's vision. The nation prospers under its great kings—Saul, David, and Solomon. But these men are all too human, and after Solomon's death civil war divides the nation. Ten of the tribes become known as Israel and two tribes become known as Judah.

During these difficult times, the people of both nations grow decadent. In response, God raises up a new breed of men—the prophets—whose impassioned pleas to return to God fill nearly one-fifth of today's Bible. The prophets—Isaiah, Jeremiah, Amos, Daniel, Hosea, Malachi, Micah, and others—are not primarily predictors of the future as we might think. Rather, they are soulful critics of the present. They remind God's people of their past and the vision of their forsaken God who continues to offer forgiveness and mercy. But their cries go unheeded.

Finally, the great empire of Assyria enslaves the ten tribes of Israel and disperses them throughout the world. The Babylonians capture Judah and raze Jerusalem. Even God's temple is destroyed. For four hundred desolate years, God's people hear nothing.

But God has not given up. He still has plans for his scattered people. After centuries of silence, he speaks in a very different way. He sends Jesus, his Son, to live among his people and to introduce a new kind of kingdom. Out of the roots of the people and nation God created, Jesus comes to proclaim the message of God's love to all the world.

Key Points of This Session

1. Despite its thousands of pages, colorful characters, and scattered locations, the Old Testament tells a single, coherent story: God created a world and a family. He loses that family, and then he gets it back!
2. When we begin to see how the Old Testament story unfolds, God's message to us becomes more understandable. Through the trials and tribulations and ups and downs of God's family, we see recurring themes of sin and repentance, forgiveness and judgment, hope and sorrow, joy and despair. We gain a greater understanding of God's love for us.

Suggested Reading

This session does not correspond to a specific chapter of *The Bible Jesus Read.* To gain a better understanding of the Bible as story concept, you may want to refer to *The Story of Stories* by Karen Hinckley, published by NavPress.

Session Outline (54 minutes)

I. Introduction (5 minutes)
   A. Welcome
   B. What's to Come
   C. Questions to Think About
II. Video Presentation: "Understanding the Old Testament" (13 minutes)
III. Group Discovery (30 minutes)
   A. Video Highlights (3 minutes)
   B. Large Group Exploration: Old Testament Overview (22 minutes)
   C. Group Discussion (5 minutes)
IV. Personal Journey (5 minutes)
V. Closing Meditation (1 minute)

Materials

You'll need a VCR, TV, and Bible. You may also find a whiteboard, flip chart, or overhead projector to be useful in guiding group discussion. View the video prior to leading the session so that you are familiar with its main points.

For this session, it would be helpful to prepare ahead for the Large Group Exploration. Write out each question and its accompanying Scripture references on a 3 x 5 card. Pass out these cards as participants enter your meeting room. If your group is very small, some participants will need to read and respond to more than one question.

SESSION TWO

Understanding the Old Testament

The Old Testament is the story of the tremendous decline—very quickly—of what God had created. It relates his slow, tedious progress to create a people, and out of that people to send his Son, who would take the same message of God's love and introduce it to all the nations of the world.

—Philip Yancey

5 min. INTRODUCTION

Welcome

Welcome participants to Session 2 of *The Bible Jesus Read* course: "Understanding the Old Testament."

What's to Come

The Old Testament is full of things God wants us to know–about himself, about ourselves, and about life. Despite the fact that it was written over a span of at least a five hundred years and that its thousands of pages reveal the stories of dozens of heroes and villains who lived in scattered locations throughout the Middle East, the Old Testament tells a single, coherent story. Philip summarizes that story in just a few words: "God creates a world and a family. He loses that family, and then he gets it back." This session highlights the ups and downs of that story, providing a context through which we can begin to understand the Old Testament.

Let's begin by considering a few questions. Please turn to page 23 of your Participant's Guide.

Questions to Think About

Participant's Guide page 23.

As time permits, ask two or more of the following questions and solicit responses from the participants.

NOTES

SESSION TWO

Understanding the Old Testament

> The Old Testament is the story of the tremendous decline—very quickly—of what God had created. It relates his slow, tedious progress to create a people, and out of that people to send his Son, who would take the same message of God's love and introduce it to all the nations of the world.
>
> —Philip Yancey

Questions to Think About

1. Think about the Old Testament reading you have done in the past. Which themes stand out to you?

2. What relationships do you see between these themes? In what ways do these relationships indicate the existence of a "bigger picture"?

3. If you were to make the Old Testament into a movie, what might you choose as the story line or plot?

23

1. Think about the Old Testament reading you have done in the past. Which themes stand out to you?

Encourage participants to share the recurring themes they already know about in the Old Testament. These might include: God's intolerance of sin, the people's seeming inability to avoid idolatry, a repeated pattern of obedience followed by disobedience, God's miraculous intervention on behalf of his people, God's longing for relationship with his people, etc. Once you grasp the "big picture" of the Old Testament, you'll find it easier to understand its parts.

Note: It would be helpful to record the group's responses to this first question on a whiteboard, flip chart, or overhead projector so that it will be easier to discuss the next question.

2. What relationships do you see between these themes? In what ways do these relationships indicate the existence of a "bigger picture"?

Encourage participants to identify connections between various themes and to look for evidence of a "story" behind those themes. For example, God's intolerance of sin is directly related to his insistence on obedience, which is explained by the "big picture" of his longing for relationship with his people.

Note: This type of thinking may be new to some participants. Be careful not to be critical of participants who do not immediately understand the concept of "story."

3. If you were to make the Old Testament into a movie, what might you choose as the story line or plot?

Responses will vary. The point is not to come up with the "right" answer, but to consider the plot that stands out to individual participants. Some may focus on the physical and spiritual journeys of God's people. Others may focus on action—the tales of the kings and the wars with the Canaanites. Some may take the story line of one of Jesus' stories, such as the story of the landowner who sent his messengers, then his son, to his rebellious tenants (Matthew 21:33–46). Still others may focus on the contrast between God's faithfulness to his people and their unfaithfulness to him.

Let's keep these ideas in mind as we view the video. There is space to take notes on page 24.

13 min. VIDEO PRESENTATION: "UNDERSTANDING THE OLD TESTAMENT"

Participant's Guide page 24.

NOTES

SESSION TWO

Understanding the Old Testament

> The Old Testament is the story of the tremendous decline—very quickly—of what God had created. It relates his slow, tedious progress to create a people, and out of that people to send his Son, who would take the same message of God's love and introduce it to all the nations of the world.
>
> —Philip Yancey

Questions to Think About

1. Think about the Old Testament reading you have done in the past. Which themes stand out to you?

2. What relationships do you see between these themes? In what ways do these relationships indicate the existence of a "bigger picture"?

3. If you were to make the Old Testament into a movie, what might you choose as the story line or plot?

23

Leader's Video Observations

The Old Testament: a single, coherent story

The Old Testament plot:

A discouraging beginning

God's new plan

God's vision is fulfilled, then fades

The prophets remind the people of God's vision

Four hundred years of silence

Jesus: a new messenger, a new kind of relationship

NOTES

Video Presentation: "Understanding the Old Testament"

The Old Testament, a single, coherent story

The Old Testament plot:
- A discouraging beginning
- God's new plan
- God's vision is fulfilled, then fades
- The prophets remind the people of God's vision
- Four hundred years of silence
- Jesus: a new messenger, a new kind of relationship

30 min. GROUP DISCOVERY

For this session, you will not break into small groups during the Group Discovery. Begin with the Video Highlights (3 minutes), then complete the Large Group Exploration (22 minutes), and wrap up your discovery time with the Group Discussion (5 minutes).

Please turn to page 25 as we discuss some questions related to the video segment we have just seen.

Video Highlights (3 minutes)

Participant's Guide page 25.

As time permits, ask one or more of the following questions, which directly relate to the video the participants have just seen.

1. Philip said, "I would express the plot like this: God creates a world and a family. He loses that family, and then he gets it back." How well does this plot match what you know of the Old Testament? In what ways does it help you to better understand the Old Testament?

Some participants may grasp the concept of plot and story right away, while others may not. Although some participants may see the Old Testament story in a different light, most will find that viewing the Old Testament as the story Philip describes helps it to make sense and makes it more approachable.

2. What role does Jesus' coming to earth after a silence of four hundred years play in the Old Testament's plot? What does this event tell us about God?

Jesus' coming continued the story; God's love and forgiveness—his mercy and grace shine all the way through the Old Testament and culminate in the coming of Jesus; God must have incredible love for us because he is so persistent and faithful in giving us a new start no matter how badly we stumble.

Perspective

The Bible's striking unity is one strong sign that God directed its composition. By using a variety of authors and cultural situations, God developed a complete record of what he wants us to know; amazingly, the parts fit together in such a way that a single story does emerge.

—Philip Yancey

NOTES

Video Highlights

1. Philip said, "I would express the plot like this: God creates a world and a family. He loses that family, and then he gets it back." How well does this plot match what you know of the Old Testament? In what ways does it help you to better understand the Old Testament?

2. What role does Jesus' coming to earth after a silence of four hundred years play in the Old Testament's plot? What does this event tell us about God?

Perspective

The Bible's striking unity is one strong sign that God directed its composition. By using a variety of authors and cultural situations, God developed a complete record of what he wants us to know; amazingly, the parts fit together in such a way that a single story does emerge.

—Philip Yancey

Now we're ready for the Large Group Exploration part of this session. Please turn to page 26.

Large Group Exploration: Old Testament Overview (22 minutes)

Participant's Guide page 26.

Read the introductory paragraph to the group, then begin discussing the questions that follow. In order to get through this material in one session, it would be helpful to write each question and its accompanying Scripture references on a 3 x 5 card. Pass out these cards as participants enter your meeting room. When you begin this part of the session, allow one to two minutes for participants to silently read their respective Scripture passages and consider their responses. Then ask participants to share their responses with the group. If your group is very small, some participants will need to read and respond to more than one question.

Our exploration time today will differ from what we did in our previous session. We're going to remain together as a large group to consider a few key highlights of the plot of the Old Testament's story. So hold onto your seats, because we have about twenty minutes to give ourselves an overview of the entire Old Testament!

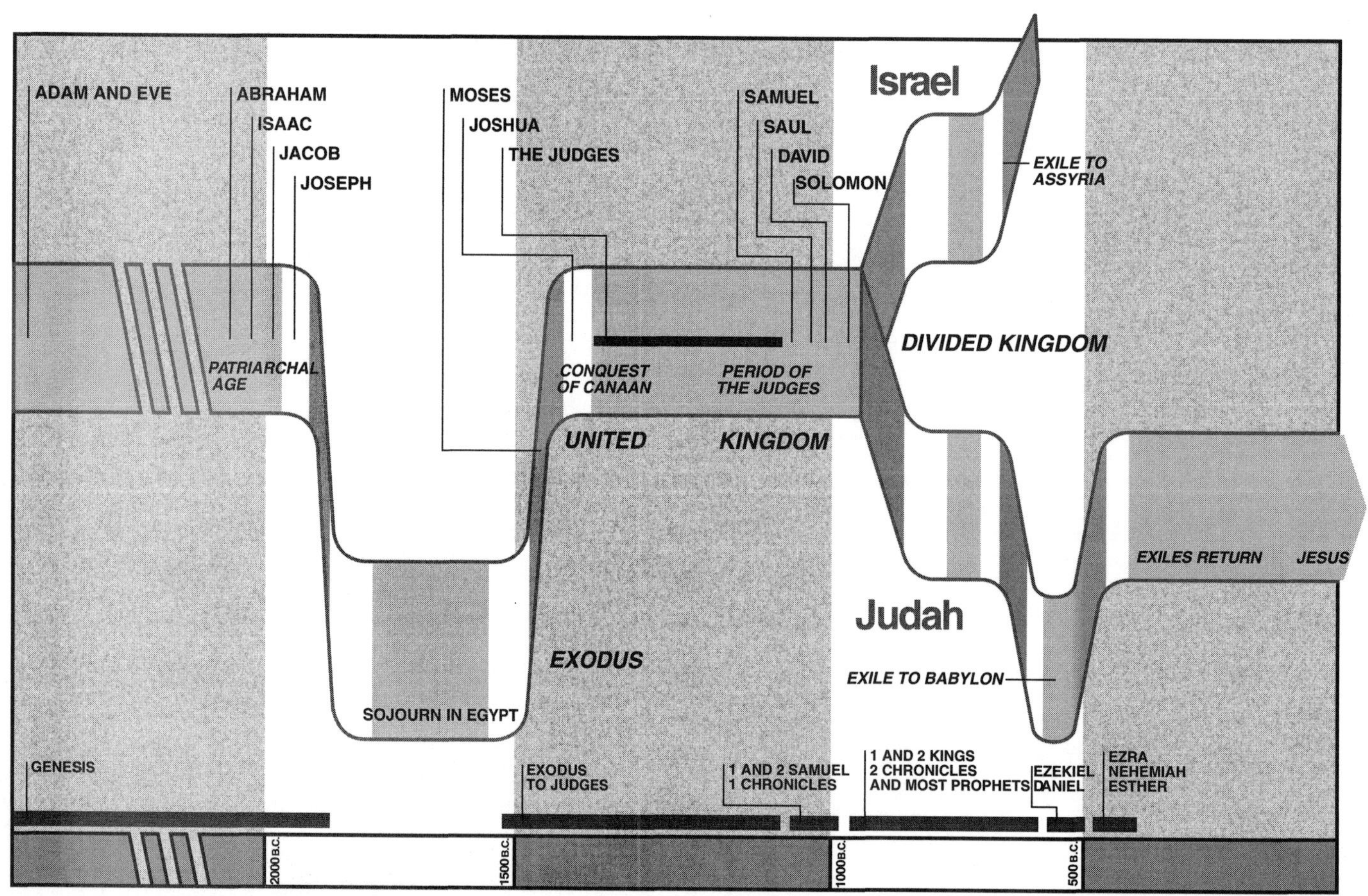

NOTES

Large Group Exploration: Old Testament Overview

Our exploration time today will differ from what we did in our previous session. We're going to remain together as a large group to consider a few key highlights of the plot of the Old Testament's story. So hold onto your seats, because we have about twenty minutes to give ourselves an overview of the entire Old Testament!

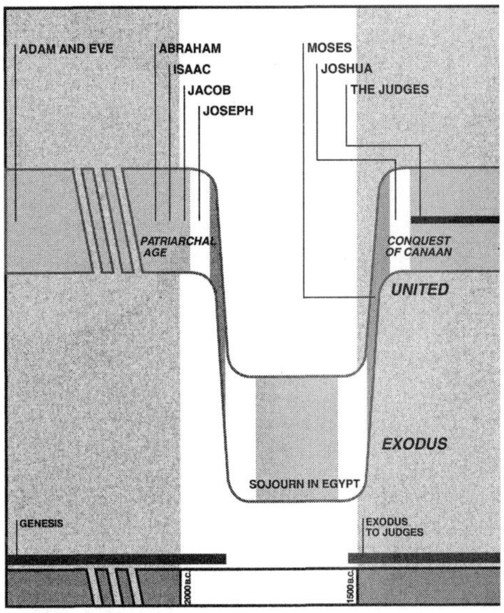

Perspective

> The Old Testament . . . does not give us a lesson in theology, with abstract concepts neatly arranged in logical order. Quite the opposite: it gives an advanced course in Life with God, expressed in a style at once personal and passionate.
>
> —Philip Yancey

God Creates a World

1. What did God have in mind for his human creation at the beginning, and what response did he receive? (See Genesis 1:27; 2:15–18; 3:1–11.)

God created man and woman for relationship with one another and for relationship with him. Their response, with the coaching of Satan, the serpent, was to violate the one condition God had placed on their relationship. When they ate the fruit of the tree that God had forbidden, they immediately understood evil, and their relationship with God (and with one another) changed forever. Whereas they had delighted in their relationship with God before, they now hid from him.

2. As Adam's family grew, what kind of relationship did Adam's descendants have with God? What was God's response? (See Genesis 6:5–8; 7:1–4; 8:15–19.)

Adam's descendants turned their back on God completely and thought about only evil things. As a result, God grieved that he had ever created humankind. Even so, God kept looking for just one person who would obey him, and he found Noah. So God saved Noah, his family, and pairs of animals and birds from the great flood that he sent to destroy the people and animals of the earth.

God Chooses a Family to Fulfill His New Plan

3. Noah had three sons—Shem, Ham, and Japheth—who fathered the nations that spread out over the earth after the flood. One of Shem's descendants was Abram, an otherwise insignificant nomad. But God singled out Abram and appeared to him. What was God's message to Abram, and what was Abram's response? (See Genesis 12:1–8.)

God promised to make Abram into a great nation, to bless him, to make his name great, to make him a blessing to other people, to bless those who blessed him, to curse those who cursed him, to bless everyone on earth through Abram. Abram picked up everything he owned and headed for the land of Canaan, as God commanded. As he went, he built altars to the Lord that expressed his relationship with God.

4. God had chosen a family to carry out his plan, but the road to fulfilling that plan was bumpy indeed. The chart below highlights a few of

NOTES

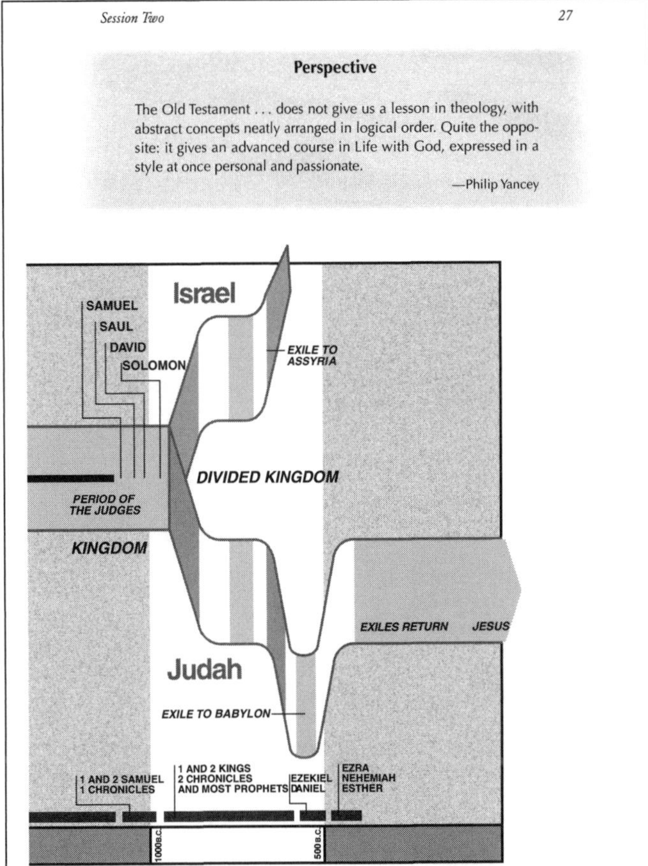

Perspective

The Old Testament . . . does not give us a lesson in theology, with abstract concepts neatly arranged in logical order. Quite the opposite: it gives an advanced course in Life with God, expressed in a style at once personal and passionate.

—Philip Yancey

God Creates a World

1. What did God have in mind for his human creation at the beginning, and what response did he receive? (See Genesis 1:27; 2:15–18; 3:1–11.)

2. As Adam's family grew, what kind of relationship did Adam's descendants have with God? What was God's response? (See Genesis 6:5–8; 7:1–4; 8:15–19.)

God Chooses a Family to Fulfill His New Plan

3. Noah had three sons—Shem, Ham, and Japheth—who fathered the nations that spread out over the earth after the flood. One of Shem's descendants was Abram, an otherwise insignificant nomad. But God singled out Abram and appeared to him. What was God's message to Abram? What was Abram's response? (See Genesis 12:1–8.)

4. God had chosen a family to carry out his plan, but the road to fulfilling that plan was bumpy indeed. The chart below highlights a few of the high points and low points. Review the chart and discuss what you would have thought God was doing at various points along the way. At which times might you have thought God had given up on his plan? At which times might you have thought God's plan was near fulfillment? Which other low and high points of Old Testament history prior to the Exodus stand out in your mind? As you see the Old Testament story unfold, what are your thoughts about God?

Reference	Low Point	High Point
Genesis 15:2–6	Sarah, Abram's wife, was barren	
Genesis 17:15–17; 21:1–7		In her old age, Sarah gave birth to Isaac
Genesis 22:1–2	God asked Abram to sacrifice Isaac	
Genesis 22:13		God provided a ram as a substitute sacrifice for Isaac
Genesis 32:28; 35:23–26; 49:1		Isaac's son, Jacob, had twelve sons who were to father the twelve tribes of Israel
Genesis 37:23–36	Jacob's ten oldest sons sold their brother Joseph as a slave and convinced Jacob that Joseph was dead	

the high points and low points. Review the chart and discuss what you would have thought God was doing at various points along the way. At which times might you have thought God had given up on his plan? At which times might you have thought God's plan was near fulfillment? Which other low and high points of Old Testament history prior to the Exodus stand out in your mind? As you see the Old Testament story unfold, what are your thoughts about God?

Reference	Low Point	High Point
Genesis 15:2–6	Sarah, Abram's wife, was barren	
Genesis 17:15–17; 21:1–7		In her old age, Sarah gave birth to Isaac
Genesis 22:1–2	God asked Abram to sacrifice Isaac	
Genesis 22:13		God provided a ram as a substitute sacrifice for Isaac
Genesis 32:28; 35:23–26; 49:1		Isaac's son Jacob had twelve sons who were to father the twelve tribes of Israel
Genesis 37:23–36	Jacob's ten oldest sons sold their brother Joseph as a slave and convinced Jacob that Joseph was dead	
Genesis 41:41–43; 42:1–2; 45:4–7		Joseph became second in command in Egypt and was able to save his family from starvation
Exodus 1:6–7		The Israelites prospered in Egypt
Exodus 1:8–14	The Egyptians eventually forgot who Joseph was and enslaved the Israelites	
Exodus 2:1–10; 3:1–10		After 430 years, God raised up Moses to bring God's people out of Egypt

God's Covenant with His People

5. What kinds of challenges did the Israelites face as they traversed the wilderness after leaving Egypt? How did they respond? How did God respond? (See Exodus 16:1–3, 11–16; 17:1–6, 8–13.)

NOTES

4. God had chosen a family to carry out his plan, but the road to fulfilling that plan was bumpy indeed. The chart below highlights a few of the high points and low points. Review the chart and discuss what you would have thought God was doing at various points along the way. At which times might you have thought God had given up on his plan? At which times might you have thought God's plan was near fulfillment? Which other low and high points of Old Testament history prior to the Exodus stand out in your mind? As you see the Old Testament story unfold, what are your thoughts about God?

Reference	Low Point	High Point
Genesis 15:2–6	Sarah, Abram's wife, was barren	
Genesis 17:15–17; 21:1–7		In her old age, Sarah gave birth to Isaac
Genesis 22:1–2	God asked Abram to sacrifice Isaac	
Genesis 22:13		God provided a ram as a substitute sacrifice for Isaac
Genesis 32:28; 35:23–26; 49:1		Isaac's son, Jacob, had twelve sons who were to father the twelve tribes of Israel
Genesis 37:23–36	Jacob's ten oldest sons sold their brother Joseph as a slave and convinced Jacob that Joseph was dead	

Reference	Low Point	High Point
Genesis 41:41–43; 42:1–2; 45:4–7		Joseph became second in command in Egypt and was able to save his family from starvation
Exodus 1:6–7		The Israelites prospered in Egypt
Exodus 1:8–14	The Egyptians eventually forgot who Joseph was and enslaved the Israelites	
Exodus 2:1–10; 3:1–10		After 430 years, God raised up Moses to bring God's people out of Egypt

God's Covenant with His People

5. What kinds of challenges did the Israelites face as they traversed the wilderness after leaving Egypt? How did they respond? How did God respond? (See Exodus 16:1–3, 11–16; 17:1–6, 8–13.)

6. Three months to the day after leaving Egypt, the Israelites camped at the foot of Mount Sinai.

   a. What message did God give to Moses and his people? (See Exodus 19:1–6.)

The Israelites were tired, hungry, and thirsty, so they complained loudly. In response, God miraculously provided bread and meat to eat and water to drink. When the Amalekites (desert tribesmen) attacked them, God delivered them. God remained faithful to them despite their sin and complaints.

6. Three months to the day after leaving Egypt, the Israelites camped at the foot of Mount Sinai.

   a. What message did God give to Moses and his people? (See Exodus 19:1–6.)

God offered to make a covenant with them, making them his treasured possession and priests among all the nations of the world if they would recognize him as their King and obey him fully.

   b. How did the people respond to God's offer by their *words* and by their *actions?* (See Exodus 24:3; 32:1–4.)

They agreed to do what God asked them to do, but soon after they gave up on God and turned to worship other gods.

   c. What was God's response to their sin? (See Exodus 32:9–14.)

God wanted to destroy them, but he listened to Moses. By his amazing grace, God forgave them and gave them another chance.

Life in the Promised Land

7. After accepting God's covenant, the people continued their journey toward Canaan. Yet, just as before, they continued to struggle with unfaithfulness, disobedience, and grumbling. Their history in receiving and settling the land God promised to them fits a "bad news, good news" pattern.

   By this point, God had made known his desire for his chosen people. Review the chart below and discuss how you think God viewed each of these circumstances. At which points would you have thought God would have given up on his plan? What does this "bad news, good news" pattern reveal to you about the heart of God?

Reference	Bad News	Good News
Numbers 13:17–30		The land of Canaan was abundantly fertile
Numbers 13:31–14:24	The people were so afraid of the giants living in Canaan's fortified cities that they wanted to stone the Isrealite leaders and go back to Egypt, which led to forty years of desert wandering	

NOTES

Genesis 41:41–43; 42:1–2; 45:4–7		Joseph became second in command in Egypt and was able to save his family from starvation
Exodus 1:6–7		The Israelites prospered in Egypt
Exodus 1:8–14	The Egyptians eventually forgot who Joseph was and enslaved the Israelites	
Exodus 2:1–10; 3:1–10		After 430 years, God raised up Moses to bring God's people out of Egypt

God's Covenant with His People

5. What kinds of challenges did the Israelites face as they traversed the wilderness after leaving Egypt? How did they respond? How did God respond? (See Exodus 16:1–3, 11–16; 17:1–6, 8–13.)

6. Three months to the day after leaving Egypt, the Israelites camped at the foot of Mount Sinai.

   a. What message did God give to Moses and his people? (See Exodus 19:1–6.)

   b. How did the people respond to God's offer by their *words* and by their *actions*? (See Exodus 24:3; 32:1–4.)

   c. What was God's response to their sin? (See Exodus 32:9–14.)

Life in the Promised Land

7. After accepting God's covenant, the people continued their journey toward Canaan. Yet, just as before, they continued to struggle with unfaithfulness, disobedience, and grumbling. Their history in receiving and settling the land God promised to them fits a "bad news, good news" pattern.

   By this point, God had made known his desire for his chosen people. Review the following chart and discuss how you think God viewed each of these circumstances. At which points would you have thought God would have given up on his plan? What does this "bad news, good news" pattern reveal to you about the heart of God?

Reference	**Bad News**	**Good News**
Numbers 13:17–30		The land of Canaan was abundantly fertile
Numbers 13:31–14:24	The people were so afraid of the giants living in Canaan's fortified cities that they wanted to stone the Isrealite leaders and go back to Egypt, which led to forty years of desert wandering	
Joshua 3:1, 5–16; 4:19–24		By God's miraculous power, the people crossed the Jordan River into Canaan
Joshua 24:11–24		Under Joshua's leadership, the people promised to serve and obey the Lord only
Judges 2:6–7, 10–15	The next generation abandoned God and worshiped the gods of the Canaanites, so God allowed their enemies to oppress them	
Judges 2:16, 18		God raised up judges to save and lead his people
Judges 2:17, 19	After each judge died, the people went back to their evil ways	
1 Samuel 8:4–20; 11:15; 12:19–20	Despite God's warnings, the people rejected God as their king and Saul became king	
1 Samuel 13:6–14	Saul disobeyed God, so God chose another person to be king	
1 Samuel 16:1, 6–13		Samuel anointed David, the Lord's choice for a new king

Reference	Bad News	Good News
Joshua 3:1, 5–16; 4:19–24		By God's miraculous power, the people crossed the Jordan River into Canaan
Joshua 24:11–24		Under Joshua's leadership, the people promised to serve and obey the Lord only
Judges 2:6–7, 10–15	The next generation abandoned God and worshiped the gods of the Canaanites, so God allowed their enemies to oppress them	
Judges 2:16, 18		God raised up judges to save and lead his people
Judges 2:17, 19	After each judge died, the people went back to their evil ways	
1 Samuel 8:4–20; 11:15; 12:19–20	Despite God's warnings, the people rejected God as their king and Saul became king	
1 Samuel 13:6–14	Saul disobeyed God, so God chose another person to be king	
1 Samuel 16:1, 6–13		Samuel anointed David, the Lord's choice for a new king
2 Samuel 5:1–7; 7:8–16		David united the nation and captured Zion (Jerusalem), and God promised that David's house would endure forever
2 Samuel 11:2–17	David stumbled, committing adultery and murder	
2 Samuel 12:1–14		Nathan confronted David with his sin and David repented
1 Kings 3:7–14; 6:1, 8; 9:1–9		Solomon became king, asked God for wisdom, and built a beautiful temple for God
1 Kings 11:1–6; 9–13	Solomon married many foreign wives who turned his heart away from God	
1 Kings 12:1–5; 12–19	Rehoboam succeeds Solomon,but the kingdom splits under his harsh rule	

NOTES

Reference	Bad News	Good News
Numbers 13:17–30		The land of Canaan was abundantly fertile
Numbers 13:31–14:24	The people were so afraid of the giants living in Canaan's fortified cities that they wanted to stone the Isrealite leaders and go back to Egypt, which led to forty years of desert wandering	
Joshua 3:1, 5–16; 4:19–24		By God's miraculous power, the people crossed the Jordan River into Canaan
Joshua 24:11–24		Under Joshua's leadership, the people promised to serve and obey the Lord only
Judges 2:6–7, 10–15	The next generation abandoned God and worshiped the gods of the Canaanites, so God allowed their enemies to oppress them	
Judges 2:16, 18		God raised up judges to save and lead his people
Judges 2:17, 19	After each judge died, the people went back to their evil ways	
1 Samuel 8:4–20; 11:15; 12:19–20	Despite God's warnings, the people rejected God as their king and Saul became king	
1 Samuel 13:6–14	Saul disobeyed God, so God chose another person to be king	
1 Samuel 16:1, 6–13		Samuel anointed David, the Lord's choice for a new king

Reference	Bad News	Good News
2 Samuel 5:1–7; 7:8–16		David united the nation and captured Zion (Jerusalem), and God promised that David's house would endure forever
2 Samuel 11:2–17	David stumbled, committing adultery and murder	
2 Samuel 12:1–14		Nathan confronted David with his sin and David repented
1 Kings 3:7–14; 6:1, 8; 9:1–9		Solomon became king, asked God for wisdom, and built a beautiful temple for God
1 Kings 11:1–6; 9–13	Solomon married many foreign wives who turned his heart away from God	
1 Kings 12:1–5; 12–19	Rehoboam succeeds Solomon, but the kingdom splits under his harsh rule	

The Cry of the Prophets

8. Almost immediately after Israel defected from Rehoboam's rule, its rulers encouraged the people to pursue evil and worship idols (1 Kings 12:26–30). King Ahab, who married Jezebel (a practicing witch and Phoenician princess), was the culmination of this evil line of kings. After Ahab built a temple to Baal (1 Kings 16:30–33), God could take no more and responded to Ahab's flagrant sinfulness. Who did God send to ask the people to choose whether they belonged to God or to Baal? What was the result? (See 1 Kings 18:15–40; 19:14–18.)

The Cry of the Prophets

8. Almost immediately after Israel defected from Rehoboam's rule, its rulers encouraged the people to pursue evil and worship idols (1 Kings 12:26–30). King Ahab, who married Jezebel (a practicing witch and Phoenician princess), was the culmination of this evil line of kings. After Ahab built a temple to Baal (1 Kings 16:30–33), God could take no more and responded to Ahab's flagrant sinfulness. Who did God send to ask the people to choose whether they belonged to God or to Baal? What was the result? (See 1 Kings 18:15–40; 19:14–18.)

Elijah came and told King Ahab to summon the people and the 850 false prophets and to meet him on Mount Carmel. There, Elijah set up a showdown between God and the false prophets. There was no doubt in the people's minds that God won. They caught and killed all the false prophets. Although the people soon returned to their evil ways, God promised Elijah that his work had not been in vain because God had preserved 7,000 faithful worshipers.

9. The spiritual condition of Israel, the northern kingdom, continued to deteriorate, so God sent prophets such as Amos and Hosea to try to turn his chosen family back to him. Ironically, God used the nation that had listened to Jonah–Assyria–to destroy stubborn Israel in the end. Prophets such as Joel, Isaiah, Micah, Habakkuk, Jeremiah, and Ezekiel spoke God's words to the people of Judah, in the south, who also grew more and more unfaithful to God. Finally, what did God allow King Nebuchadnezzar of Babylon to do? (See 2 Kings 25:8–21.)

King Nebuchadnezzar conquered Jerusalem on August 14, 586 B.C. He burned God's temple, the palace, and all the houses and important buildings. He broke down the walls, executed the leading priests and chief officials, and took almost everyone to Babylon.

10. Even while God's people were in exile, Satan was working to destroy God's plan. The book of Esther exposes yet another attack by Satan against God's chosen family. What was the threat, and how was it resolved? (See Esther 3:5–14; 8:3–8, 11.)

Haman arranged for a royal edict by which every Jew in the Persian Empire would be killed. This would have destroyed the line of David. Since there was no changing a royal edict, Queen Esther pleaded with the king and was allowed to write a corresponding royal edict that gave the Jews the right to defend themselves. Practically speaking, the second edict canceled out the first edict.

11. Such Old Testament books as Ezra, Haggai, and Zechariah record what happened to the Jews after their return to Jerusalem from captivity. Malachi, the last prophet recorded in the Old Testament, saw that the Jews in Judah doubted God's love for them, questioned his justice, and

NOTES

2 Samuel 5:1–7; 7:8–16		David united the nation and captured Zion (Jerusalem), and God promised that David's house would endure forever
2 Samuel 11:2–17	David stumbled, committing adultery and murder	
2 Samuel 12:1–14		Nathan confronted David with his sin and David repented
1 Kings 3:7–14; 6:1, 8; 9:1–9		Solomon became king, asked God for wisdom, and built a beautiful temple for God
1 Kings 11:1–6; 9–13	Solomon married many foreign wives who turned his heart away from God	
1 Kings 12:1–5; 12–19	Rehoboam succeeds Solomon, but the kingdom splits under his harsh rule	

The Cry of the Prophets

8. Almost immediately after Israel defected from Rehoboam's rule, its rulers encouraged the people to pursue evil and worship idols (1 Kings 12:26–30). King Ahab, who married Jezebel (a practicing witch and Phoenician princess), was the culmination of this evil line of kings. After Ahab built a temple to Baal (1 Kings 16:30–33), God could take no more and responded to Ahab's flagrant sinfulness. Who did God send to ask the people to choose whether they belonged to God or to Baal? What was the result? (See 1 Kings 18:15–40; 19:14–18.)

9. The spiritual condition of Israel, the northern kingdom, continued to deteriorate, so God sent prophets such as Amos and Hosea to try to turn his chosen family back to him. Ironically, God used the nation that had listened to Jonah—Assyria—to destroy stubborn Israel in the end. Prophets such as Joel, Isaiah, Micah, Habakkuk, Jeremiah, and Ezekiel spoke God's words to the people of Judah, in the south, who also grew more and more unfaithful to God. Finally, what did God allow King Nebuchadnezzar of Babylon to do? (See 2 Kings 25:8–21.)

10. Even while God's people were in exile, Satan was working to destroy God's plan. The book of Esther exposes yet another attack by Satan against God's chosen family. What was the threat, and how was it resolved? (See Esther 3:5–14; 8:3–8, 11.)

11. Such Old Testament books as Ezra, Haggai, and Zechariah record what happened to the Jews after their return to Jerusalem from captivity. Malachi, the last prophet recorded in the Old Testament, saw that the Jews in Judah doubted God's love for them, questioned his justice, and were content to pursue evil (Malachi 1:2; 2:10–12; 3:5–7, 13–14). He spoke out prophetically, but for the most part was ignored. So for four hundred years God was silent, until he brought his plan of redemption into being. What do you notice in Matthew 1 in light of the study we've just done? (Note particularly verses 1 and 17.)

were content to pursue evil (Malachi 1:2; 2:10–12; 3:5–7, 13–14). He spoke out prophetically, but for the most part was ignored. So for four hundred years God was silent, until he brought his plan of redemption into being. What do you notice in Matthew 1 in light of the study we've just done? (Note particularly verses 1 and 17.)

In this genealogy of Jesus, we see some of the names we have just read about in this short Bible study. This genealogy records the key players in the story of the Old Testament that culminates in Jesus' birth.

The Old Testament Points to Jesus!

The Old Testament has many prophecies of a coming Messiah that were fulfilled by Jesus.

Prophecy of a Coming Messiah	**Fulfillment by Jesus**
Would descend from the tribe of Judah (Genesis 49:10)	He descended from the tribe of Judah (Luke 3:33)
Would be heir to the throne of David (Isaiah 9:7)	He was in the lineage of David (Matthew 1:1, 6)
Would be born in Bethlehem (Micah 5:2)	He was born in Bethlehem (Matthew 2:1)
Daniel tells when the "Anointed One" would come (Daniel 9:25)	He was born during the days of Caesar Augustus (Luke 2:1–2)
Would be born of a virgin (Isaiah 7:14)	He was born of a virgin (Matthew 1:18)
Would minister in Galilee (Isaiah 9:1–2)	He ministered in Galilee (Matthew 4:12–16)
Would be a prophet (Deuteronomy 18:15)	He was a prophet (John 6:14)
Would enter triumphantly into Jerusalem (Zechariah 9:9)	He entered Jerusalem triumphantly (John 12:12–15)
Would be betrayed by a friend (Psalm 41:9)	He was betrayed by Judas (Mark 14:10)
Would be sold for thirty pieces of silver (Zechariah 11:13)	He was sold by Judas for thirty pieces of silver (Matthew 26:15)
Would be struck and spit upon (Isaiah 50:6)	Jews struck him and spit upon him (Mark 14:65; John 19:1–3)
Soldiers would cast lots for his clothes (Psalm 22:18)	Soldiers cast lots for his clothes (Mark 15:24)
Would be resurrected from the dead (Psalm 16:10)	He was resurrected from the dead (Matthew 28:5–9; Luke 24:36–48)
Would ascend to heaven (Psalm 68:18)	He ascended to heaven (Luke 24:50–51)

Now let's wrap up our Group Discovery time. Please turn to page 37.

NOTES

11. Such Old Testament books as Ezra, Haggai, and Zechariah record what happened to the Jews after their return to Jerusalem from captivity. Malachi, the last prophet recorded in the Old Testament, saw that the Jews in Judah doubted God's love for them, questioned his justice, and were content to pursue evil (Malachi 1:2; 2:10–12; 3:5–7, 13–14). He spoke out prophetically, but for the most part was ignored. So for four hundred years God was silent, until he brought his plan of redemption into being. What do you notice in Matthew 1 in light of the study we've just done? (Note particularly verses 1 and 17.)

The Old Testament Points to Jesus!

The Old Testament has many prophecies of a coming Messiah that were fulfilled by Jesus.

Prophecy of a Coming Messiah	Fulfillment by Jesus
Would descend from the tribe of Judah (Genesis 49:10)	He descended from the tribe of Judah (Luke 3:33)
Would be heir to the throne of David (Isaiah 9:7)	He was in the lineage of David (Matthew 1:1, 6)
Would be born in Bethlehem (Micah 5:2)	He was born in Bethlehem (Matthew 2:1)
Daniel tells when the "Anointed One" would come (Daniel 9:25)	He was born during the days of Caesar Augustus (Luke 2:1–2)
Would be born of a virgin (Isaiah 7:14)	He was born of a virgin (Matthew 1:18)
Would minister in Galilee (Isaiah 9:1–2)	He ministered in Galilee (Matthew 4:12–16)
Would be a prophet (Deuteronomy 18:15)	He was a prophet (John 6:14)
Would enter triumphantly into Jerusalem (Zechariah 9:9)	He entered Jerusalem triumphantly (John 12:12–15)
Would be betrayed by a friend (Psalm 41:9)	He was betrayed by Judas (Mark 14:10)
Would be sold for thirty pieces of silver (Zechariah 11:13)	He was sold by Judas for thirty pieces of silver (Matthew 26:15)
Would be struck and spit upon (Isaiah 50:6)	Jews struck him and spit upon him (Mark 14:65; John 19:1–3)
Soldiers would cast lots for his clothes (Psalm 22:18)	Soldiers cast lots for his clothes (Mark 15:24)
Would be resurrected from the dead (Psalm 16:10)	He was resurrected from the dead (Matthew 28:5–9; Luke 24:36–48)
Would ascend to heaven (Psalm 68:18)	He ascended to heaven (Luke 24:50–51)

Group Discussion (5 minutes)

Participant's Guide page 37.

Use one or more of the following questions to encourage participants to share their observations with the entire group.

If your Large Group Exploration ran long, you may choose to skip this discussion and move directly to the Personal Journey segment.

1. As you've seen a little bit of the Old Testament story unfold, what new things are you seeing in the Old Testament that you have not seen before?
2. In what ways do you better understand Philip Yancey's summation of the Old Testament's story line: "God creates a world and a family. He loses that family, and then he gets it back"?

Now it's time for each of us to consider on a personal level what we've been discussing and thinking about. Please turn to page 38.

Did You Know?

I find it remarkable that this diverse collection of manuscripts written over a period of a millennium by several dozen authors possesses as much unity as it does. To appreciate this feat, imagine a book begun five hundred years before Columbus and just now completed!

—Philip Yancey

5 min. PERSONAL JOURNEY: TO BEGIN NOW

Participant's Guide page 38.

When we begin to see how the Old Testament story unfolds, God's message to us becomes more understandable. Through the trials and tribulations and ups and downs of God's family, we see recurring themes of sin and repentance, forgiveness and judgment, hope and sorrow, joy and despair. We discover a greater understanding of God's love for us—a fuller picture of his mercy and patient longsuffering.

Take some time now by yourself to consider what you have discovered in this session and how it applies to your daily life.

NOTES

Group Discussion

1. As you've seen a little bit of the Old Testament story unfold, what new things are you seeing in the Old Testament that you have not seen before?

2. In what ways do you better understand Philip Yancey's summation of the Old Testament's story line: "God creates a world and a family. He loses that family, and then he gets it back"?

Did You Know?

I find it remarkable that this diverse collection of manuscripts written over a period of a millennium by several dozen authors possesses as much unity as it does. To appreciate this feat, imagine a book begun five hundred years before Columbus and just now completed!

—Philip Yancey

Personal Journey: To Begin Now

When we begin to see how the Old Testament story unfolds, God's message to us becomes more understandable. Through the trials and tribulations and ups and downs of God's family, we see recurring themes of sin and repentance, forgiveness and judgment, hope and sorrow, joy and despair. We discover a greater understanding of God's love for us—a fuller picture of his mercy and patient longsuffering.

Take some time by yourself to consider what you have discovered in this session and how it applies to your daily life.

1. Write a short, personal summary of how your understanding of the Old Testament or the God of the Old Testament has grown today. If you aren't sure how to start, use the following questions as a guide:

   In what ways do you feel you know God better now than when you got up this morning?

   What did you learn about God that awed or surprised you today?

   How would you describe the Old Testament story in a sentence or two?

   What surprised you about what you discovered today?

1. Write a short, personal summary of how your understanding of the Old Testament or the God of the Old Testament has grown today. If you aren't sure how to start, use the following questions as a guide:

   In what ways do you feel you know God better now than when you got up this morning?

   What did you learn about God that awed or surprised you today?

   How would you describe the Old Testament story in a sentence or two?

   What surprised you about what you discovered today?

Perspective

When I see God working with individual human beings, it's amazing what he puts up with. God can take anything as long as his people turn back to him and let him pick them up. We fall down, we get up. We fall down, we get up. All the way through the Old Testament I see pictures of that grace. God forgives. He gives people a new start. That God of mercy and grace shines all the way through the Old Testament.

—Philip Yancey

2. As you consider the ups and downs of the Old Testament history of God's chosen people, what messages do you find that are relevant to you? In what ways do you see your relationship with God reflected in the Old Testament stories? How might that affect your relationship with God from now on?

Let participants know when there is 1 minute remaining. Remind participants that they may want to continue their journey by completing the additional exercise on page 40 of their Participant's Guide before the next session.

PERSONAL JOURNEY: TO DO BETWEEN SESSIONS

As the title of Philip's book expresses, the Old Testament *is* the Bible Jesus read. He prayed its prayers. Memorized its poems. Sang its songs. Heard its stories. Pondered its prophecies. He also used phrases from the Old Testament to define himself and traced in its passages every important fact about himself and his mission. The more we comprehend the Old Testament, the more we comprehend him.

NOTES

Personal Journey: To Begin Now

When we begin to see how the Old Testament story unfolds, God's message to us becomes more understandable. Through the trials and tribulations and ups and downs of God's family, we see recurring themes of sin and repentance, forgiveness and judgment, hope and sorrow, joy and despair. We discover a greater understanding of God's love for us—a fuller picture of his mercy and patient longsuffering.

Take some time by yourself to consider what you have discovered in this session and how it applies to your daily life.

1. Write a short, personal summary of how your understanding of the Old Testament or the God of the Old Testament has grown today. If you aren't sure how to start, use the following questions as a guide:

   In what ways do you feel you know God better now than when you got up this morning?

   What did you learn about God that awed or surprised you today?

   How would you describe the Old Testament story in a sentence or two?

   What surprised you about what you discovered today?

Summary:

Perspective

When I see God working with individual human beings, it's amazing what he puts up with. God can take anything as long as his people turn back to him and let him pick them up. We fall down, we get up. We fall down, we get up. All the way through the Old Testament I see pictures of that grace. God forgives. He gives people a new start. That God of mercy and grace shines all the way through the Old Testament.

—Philip Yancey

2. As you consider the ups and downs of the Old Testament history of God's chosen people, what messages do you find that are relevant to you? In what ways do you see your relationship with God reflected in the Old Testament stories? How might that affect your relationship with God from now on?

Personal Journey: To Do between Sessions

As the title of Philip's book expresses, the Old Testament *is* the Bible Jesus read. He prayed its prayers. Memorized its poems. Sang its songs. Heard its stories. Pondered its prophecies. He also used phrases from the Old Testament to define himself and traced in its passages every important fact about himself and his mission. The more we comprehend the Old Testament, the more we comprehend him.

1. In what ways has your understanding of who Jesus is and what he came to earth to accomplish grown as a result of this session?

2. What will you do to draw closer to the God who reveals himself through the pages of the Old Testament?

3. Take a look at the charts provided for Questions 4 and 7 of your Large Group Exploration time. To gain a deeper understanding of exactly what occurred, read the passages indicated. As you read, take particular note of the interaction between God and his people and the responses of both.

Before the next session, set aside time away from distractions to do the following exercise.

1. In what ways has your understanding of who Jesus is and what he came to earth to accomplish grown as a result of this session?
2. What will you do to draw closer to the God who reveals himself through the pages of the Old Testament?
3. Take a look at the charts provided for Questions 4 and 7 of your Large Group Exploration time. To gain a deeper understanding of exactly what occurred, read the passages indicated. As you read, take particular note of the interaction between God and his people and the responses of both.

1 min. CLOSING MEDITATION

Let's take a moment to close in prayer.

Dear God, thank you for what we have learned today about you and your praiseworthy deeds. You patiently love us despite our sinfulness, just as you loved the Israelites who willfully put you to the test and refused to obey you despite everything you did for them. Please help us to trust in you, our Rock and our Redeemer. You are the same God who provided everything the Hebrews needed in the wilderness, and you still provide for us today. Please help us to be faithful to you, to honor you with our words, our thoughts, and our actions. Draw close to us today and remind each of us of your deep love, mercy, and holiness. Amen.

—Prayer inspired by Psalm 78:1–38

NOTES

Personal Journey: To Do between Sessions

As the title of Philip's book expresses, the Old Testament *is* the Bible Jesus read. He prayed its prayers. Memorized its poems. Sang its songs. Heard its stories. Pondered its prophecies. He also used phrases from the Old Testament to define himself and traced in its passages every important fact about himself and his mission. The more we comprehend the Old Testament, the more we comprehend him.

1. In what ways has your understanding of who Jesus is and what he came to earth to accomplish grown as a result of this session?

2. What will you do to draw closer to the God who reveals himself through the pages of the Old Testament?

3. Take a look at the charts provided for Questions 4 and 7 of your Large Group Exploration time. To gain a deeper understanding of exactly what occurred, read the passages indicated. As you read, take particular note of the interaction between God and his people and the responses of both.

SESSION THREE

Job:
Seeing in the Dark

BEFORE YOU LEAD

Synopsis

This session provides a fresh look at Job, an honest, faithful, and godly man who woke up one day to find himself immersed in a maelstrom of incredible suffering. Most of us think that Job's story is about the problem of suffering, and to a certain extent it is. But Philip Yancey will open our eyes to another message in this book. "I have concluded that Job is not about the problem of pain at all," he writes. "Details of suffering serve as the ingredients of the story, but seen as a whole, the book of Job is about faith, the story of one man selected to undergo a staggering ordeal by trial. His response presents a message that applies not just to suffering people, but to every person who lives on planet Earth."

As the story unfolds, God permits Job to experience all sorts of suffering. He loses virtually all of his material possessions. His children die. His servants are killed. His body is tormented by disease. As spectators of this cosmic drama, we know in advance the reason for Job's ordeal. We know all about Satan's "bet" that Job honors God only because of the material blessings Job receives from God. We know that the key question is not *why* Job suffers but *how* Job will respond toward God when every good reason for believing in him is taken away.

Job and his friends, however, are given no explanation for Job's trials. So, just as we do when we face adversity, Job and his friends attempt to figure out the cause. Job questions why God does what he does, in effect putting God on trial. Job's three friends, in turn, cross-examine Job. They use their best arguments to convince him that a just, loving, and powerful God follows certain rules—rewarding those who do good and punishing those who do evil. They self-righteously conclude that Job's suffering must be a result of his sin.

Many of us can relate to Job's questions because we too have suffered. We have tried to make sense out of our trials. We have asked, "God, why did you allow this to happen?" We have looked backward and inward, searching for the cause of our troubles. If we learn just one thing from the book of Job, it is that "Why?" is not the main question.

God never answered the "Why?" question for Job, and he doesn't do so for us. Instead, God poses a far more important question: "Will you trust me, even in this?" This is the question on which our faith hinges. Even Job's wife, infamous for her diabolical advice to "curse God and die," recognized the real question: "Will we cling to our faith in God when faith seems impossible?"

What is remarkable about Job is that he held tightly to his faith in God and did so with integrity. Job didn't put on the cheery face so many of us think God wants from us. He didn't buy into his friends' pet theories about why bad things happen. Instead, Job grappled with the confusion and pain of his situation. With eloquent passion and honesty, Job expressed his anguish, fears, questions, and doubts to God. And God honored Job because of it.

Job's faith made a cosmic difference. He chose to live with the uncomfortable paradox that God still loved him despite all the evidence to the contrary. And we have to make the same choice. God doesn't twist our arms and force us to place our faith in him, but he cares very much how we respond to our distress. When we choose to trust God–to respond in faith when it seems impossible–God is pleased.

Key Points of This Session

1. The story of Job is a drama of cosmic proportions presented through the context of suffering. But while the theme of suffering is woven into the fabric of the story, the story of Job isn't actually about undeserved suffering. It is about having faith in God when faith seems impossible.
2. The big question of Job's drama isn't *why* we suffer, but *how* we respond to suffering. The "behind the curtain" glimpse of Job's ordeal that the Bible gives us reveals that in God's plan suffering can serve a higher good. Just as God allowed Job's suffering to occur in order to refute Satan's challenge (which called into question the entire human experiment), God continues to use suffering in ways we may not be able to see or understand.
3. The book of Job affirms that God hears our cries and is in control of this world no matter how bad things may appear to be. God did not answer all of Job's questions, but in God's presence Job's doubts melted away, and that was enough.

Suggested Reading

This session corresponds to Chapter 2 of *The Bible Jesus Read.* You may want to read this chapter in order to deepen your understanding of this material.

Session Outline (53 minutes)

I. Introduction (5 minutes)
  A. Welcome
  B. What's to Come
  C. Questions to Think About
II. Video Presentation: "Job: Seeing in the Dark" (14 minutes)
III. Group Discovery (28 minutes)
  A. Video Highlights (3 minutes)
  B. Large Group Exploration: Peeking "Behind the Curtain" as Job's Story Unfolds (8 minutes)
  C. Small Group Exploration: A Test of Faith (12 minutes)
  D. Group Discussion (5 minutes)
IV. Personal Journey (5 minutes)
V. Closing Meditation (1 minute)

Materials

You'll need a VCR, TV, and Bible. You may also find a whiteboard, flip chart, or overhead projector to be a useful tool in guiding group discussion. View the video prior to leading the session so you are familiar with its main points.

SESSION THREE

Job: Seeing in the Dark

> Job does in fact focus on the problem of suffering, but in a most unexpected way. It brilliantly asks the questions we most urgently want answered, then turns aside to propose another way of looking at the problem entirely. Like most of the Old Testament, Job at first frustrates, by refusing the simple answers we think we want, and then oddly satisfies, by pointing us in a new direction marked by flagrant realism and a tantalizing glimpse of hope.
>
> —Philip Yancey

5 min. INTRODUCTION

Welcome

Welcome participants to Session 3 of *The Bible Jesus Read* course: "Job: Seeing in the Dark."

What's to Come

This session and the sessions that follow will direct our attention to specific individuals and portions of the Old Testament. During this session, we'll take a fresh look at Job, an honest, faithful, and godly man who woke up one day to find himself immersed in a maelstrom of incredible suffering. Most of us think that Job's story is about the problem of suffering, and to a certain extent it is. But Philip Yancey will open our eyes to another message in this book. "I have concluded that Job is not about the problem of pain at all," he writes. "Details of suffering serve as the ingredients of the story, but seen as a whole, the book of Job is about faith, the story of one man selected to undergo a staggering ordeal by trial. His response presents a message that applies not just to suffering people, but to every person who lives on planet Earth."

Let's begin by considering a few questions. Please turn to page 41 of your Participant's Guide.

NOTES

SESSION THREE

Job: Seeing in the Dark

> Job does in fact focus on the problem of suffering, but in a most unexpected way. It brilliantly asks the questions we most urgently want answered, then turns aside to propose another way of looking at the problem entirely. Like most of the Old Testament, Job at first frustrates, by refusing the simple answers we think we want, and then oddly satisfies, by pointing us in a new direction marked by flagrant realism and a tantalizing glimpse of hope.
>
> —Philip Yancey

Questions to Think About

1. What words first come to mind when someone mentions the book of Job?

2. In what ways have you felt like Job? How do you respond to God when you can't figure out why God is allowing hard times in your life or in the life of someone you love? In what ways do you find it easy or difficult to be honest with God about your thoughts and feelings?

3. How do you think God views our suffering?

Questions to Think About

Participant's Guide page 41.

As time permits, ask two or more of the following questions and solicit responses from the participants.

1. What words first come to mind when someone mentions the book of Job?

View this question as a word-association exercise. Responses will vary and may include: suffering, critical friends, arrogance, bad advice, sorrow, misery, confusion, etc. The objective is for participants to express some of their preconceived notions about the book.

2. In what ways have you felt like Job? How do you respond to God when you can't figure out why God is allowing hard times in your life or in the life of someone you love? In what ways do you find it easy or difficult to be honest with God about your thoughts and feelings?

When we face adversity, we respond to God in different ways. Some of us become angry, others doubt God or accuse him of being unloving and uncaring. Some of us withdraw from him while others of us draw closer to him. Encourage participants to express and explain their views. Then explore why some of us choose to put on a "show" for God rather than being really honest with him.

3. How do you think God views our suffering?

Responses will vary greatly. Some participants may say God views our suffering as something we deserve because of our sin. Others may say suffering is a way God disciplines us, a way he teaches us important lessons. Some may say we suffer because God is testing our faith. Still others may say God is pained and grieved by our suffering.

Let's keep these ideas in mind as we view the video. There is space to take notes on page 42.

14 min. VIDEO PRESENTATION: "JOB: SEEING IN THE DARK"

Participant's Guide page 42.

Leader's Video Observations

What's the real question?

NOTES

SESSION THREE

Job: Seeing in the Dark

> Job does in fact focus on the problem of suffering, but in a most unexpected way. It brilliantly asks the questions we most urgently want answered, then turns aside to propose another way of looking at the problem entirely. Like most of the Old Testament, Job at first frustrates, by refusing the simple answers we think we want, and then oddly satisfies, by pointing us in a new direction marked by flagrant realism and a tantalizing glimpse of hope.
>
> —Philip Yancey

Questions to Think About

1. What words first come to mind when someone mentions the book of Job?

2. In what ways have you felt like Job? How do you respond to God when you can't figure out why God is allowing hard times in your life or in the life of someone you love? In what ways do you find it easy or difficult to be honest with God about your thoughts and feelings?

3. How do you think God views our suffering?

Video Presentation: "Job: Seeing in the Dark"

What's the real question?

Who is really on trial?

The question of faith: Can this be turned into good?

Living honestly with unanswered questions

How we respond to our distress matters to God

Who is really on trial?

The question of faith: Can this be turned into good?

Living honestly with unanswered questions

How we respond to our distress matters to God

28 min. GROUP DISCOVERY

If your group has seven or more members, use the Video Highlights with the entire group (3 minutes), then complete the Large Group Exploration (8 minutes), and then break into small groups of three to five people for the Small Group Exploration (12 minutes). Finally, bring everyone together for the closing Group Discussion (5 minutes).

If your group has fewer than seven members, begin with the Video Highlights (3 minutes), then complete both the Large Group Exploration (8 minutes) and the Small Group Exploration (12 minutes) as a group. Wrap up your discovery time with the Group Discussion (5 minutes).

Please turn to page 43 as we discuss some questions related to the video segment we have just seen.

Video Highlights (3 minutes)

Participant's Guide page 43.

NOTES

42 The Bible Jesus Read Participant's Guide

Video Presentation: "Job: Seeing in the Dark"

What's the real question?

Who is really on trial?

The question of faith: Can this be turned into good?

Living honestly with unanswered questions

How we respond to our distress matters to God

As time permits, ask one or more of the following questions, which directly relate to the video the participants have just seen.

1. In what ways has this video challenged your thinking on why bad things happen to good people? Explain why you agree or disagree with Philip Yancey's conclusion that how we respond to suffering is the real issue.

Encourage participants to identify and evaluate their views of why bad things happen and to do the same with Philip Yancey's conclusion. Some may believe that good things happen to good people. Others may believe that no one is perfect, so we deserve some of the bad things that happen to us. Still others may believe that bad things are going to happen no matter how "bad" or "good" we are. For some, the emphasis on how we respond to suffering as opposed to what we do to "fix" it will be a venture into new territory.

2. One of Philip Yancey's conclusions from the book of Job is that "God cares more about our faith than our pleasure." How do you respond to that conclusion, and what are its implications for your life?

The key here is to encourage participants to think about their faith and its importance to God. Some participants will agree wholeheartedly with this conclusion, and some will be troubled by the implication that God would actually allow believers to suffer in order to accomplish his goals.

Now we're ready for the Large Group Exploration part of this session. Please turn to page 44.

Large Group Exploration: Peeking "Behind the Curtain" as Job's Story Unfolds (8 minutes)

Participant's Guide page 44.

Read the introductory paragraphs to the group, then begin discussing the questions that follow.

Philip Yancey found it helpful to think of the book of Job as a mystery play, a "whodunit" detective story. "We in the audience have showed up early for a press conference in which the director explains his work (chapters 1–2)," he writes. "We learn in advance who did what in the play, and we understand that the personal drama on earth has its origin in a cosmic drama in heaven—the contest over Job's faith."

As Job's story unfolds, we—the audience—know the answers. We know that Job isn't being punished. We know that God is using him to prove to Satan that a human being's faith can be genuine and selfless. We know everything—except how Job will respond. The actors in the play, however, have no knowledge of what's to come or why things are happening. Like many other Old Testament stories, their stories reveal much about God and what it means to be a human being in relationship with God. Let's quickly review this story and see what we discover.

NOTES

Video Highlights

1. In what ways has this video challenged your thinking on why bad things happen to good people? Explain why you agree or disagree with Philip Yancey's conclusion that how we respond to suffering is the real issue.

2. One of Philip Yancey's conclusions from the book of Job is that "God cares more about our faith than our pleasure." How do you respond to that conclusion, and what are its implications for your life?

Large Group Exploration: Peeking "Behind the Curtain" as Job's Story Unfolds

Philip Yancey found it helpful to think of the book of Job as a mystery play, a "whodunit" detective story. "We in the audience have showed up early for a press conference in which the director explains his work (chapters 1–2)," he writes. "We learn in advance who did what in the play, and we understand that the personal drama on earth has its origin in a cosmic drama in heaven–the contest over Job's faith."

As Job's story unfolds, we–the audience–know the answers. We know that Job isn't being punished. We know that God is using him to prove to Satan that a human being's faith can be genuine and selfless. We know everything–except how Job will respond. The actors in the play, however, have no knowledge of what's to come or why things are happening. Like many other Old Testament stories, their stories reveal much about God and what it means to be a human being in relationship with God. Let's quickly review this story and see what we discover.

The Contest between Satan and God

God's Position	Satan's Challenge
God is worthy of love simply because of who he is, not what he does. People follow him because they love him, not because they are "bribed" to do so.	Job loves God only because he receives blessings from God. God is not worthy of love in himself.
Job has faith in God apart from God's blessings.	Job will abandon his "faith" in God as soon as the blessings disappear.
Job's faith is not a result of environmental manipulation. He will choose to believe in God despite what happens to him.	Human beings are not really free to believe, to exercise faith in God. Faith is just a product of environment and circumstances.

The Contest between Satan and God

God's Position	Satan's Challenge
God is worthy of love simply because of who he is, not what he does. People follow him because they love him, not because they are "bribed" to do so.	Job loves God only because he receives blessings from God. God is not worthy of love in himself.
Job has faith in God apart from God's blessings.	Job will abandon his "faith" in God as soon as the blessings disappear.
Job's faith is not a result of environmental manipulation. He will choose to believe in God despite what happens to him.	Human beings are not really free to believe, to exercise faith in God. Faith is just a product of environment and circumstances.

1. Read the following passages from Job 1–2 and note what each reveals about the main characters and plot of the drama that unfolds.

   a. What do we know about Job? (See Job 1:1–5.)

Job was godly, blameless, and stayed away from evil. He had a large, close-knit family, vast wealth, and was well known and respected. The "greatest" man in the entire area, Job took his relationship with God seriously.

   b. What do we know about Satan, his argument with God, and the results? (See Job 1:6–12; 2:1–7.)

Satan roams the earth, seeking to do his evil work. When talking with God, Satan said that Job loved God only because God protected him and blessed him. Satan believed at first that Job's faith would crumble if the material blessings vanished and later that Job would curse God if his health failed. In both instances, God allowed Satan to torment Job, and Job's faith and trust in God remained. It's important to remember that although Satan has the power to do evil, he can do so only within the boundaries God allows.

   c. What bad things happened to Job? (See Job 1:13–22; 2:7–10.)

A raiding party stole his oxen and donkeys and killed his servants; fire from heaven killed all his sheep and more servants; a raiding party stole his camels and killed more servants; and a wind collapsed a house, killing all of his children. Job was afflicted with painful sores all over his body. Despite all of this, Job kept his faith and didn't blame God.

   d. Who came to be with Job, and what was their initial response? (See Job 2:11–13.)

Three friends—Eliphaz, Bildad, and Zophar. They were shocked and grieved by his condition and sat with Job for a week without speaking to him.

NOTES

Large Group Exploration: Peeking "Behind the Curtain" as Job's Story Unfolds

Philip Yancey found it helpful to think of the book of Job as a mystery play, a "whodunit" detective story. "We in the audience have showed up early for a press conference in which the director explains his work (chapters 1–2)," he writes. "We learn in advance who did what in the play, and we understand that the personal drama on earth has its origin in a cosmic drama in heaven—the contest over Job's faith."

As Job's story unfolds, we—the audience—know the answers. We know that Job isn't being punished. We know that God is using him to prove to Satan that a human being's faith can be genuine and selfless. We know everything—except how Job will respond. The actors in the play, however, have no knowledge of what's to come or why things are happening. Like many other Old Testament stories, their stories reveal much about God and what it means to be a human being in relationship with God. Let's quickly review this story and see what we discover.

The Contest between Satan and God

God's Position	Satan's Challenge
God is worthy of love simply because of who he is, not what he does. People follow him because they love him, not because they are "bribed" to do so.	Job loves God only because he receives blessings from God. God is not worthy of love in himself.
Job has faith in God apart from God's blessings.	Job will abandon his "faith" in God as soon as the blessings disappear.
Job's faith is not a result of environmental manipulation. He will choose to believe in God despite what happens to him.	Human beings are not really free to believe, to exercise faith in God. Faith is just a product of environment and circumstances.

1. Read the following passages from Job 1–2 and note what each reveals about the main characters and plot of the drama that unfolds.
   a. What do we know about Job? (See Job 1:1–5.)
   b. What do we know about Satan, his argument with God, and the results? (See Job 1:6–12; 2:1–7.)
   c. What bad things happened to Job? (See Job 1:13–22; 2:7–10.)
   d. Who came to be with Job, and what was their initial response? (See Job 2:11–13.)

Perspective

Job prefers to live with an agonizing paradox, that God still loves him even though all evidence points against it. His friends laid out the logic: *Suffering comes from God. God is just. Therefore you, Job, are guilty.* After examining his own life, and toying with the notion of an unjust God, Job arrives at a different formula that on the surface makes no sense: *Suffering comes from God. God is just. I am innocent.* In the best Hebrew tradition, Job clings to all three of those truths no matter how contradictory they seem.

—Philip Yancey

Perspective

Job prefers to live with an agonizing paradox, that God still loves him even though all evidence points against it. His friends laid out the logic: *Suffering comes from God. God is just. Therefore you, Job, are guilty.* After examining his own life, and toying with the notion of an unjust God, Job arrives at a different formula that on the surface makes no sense: *Suffering comes from God. God is just. I am innocent.* In the best Hebrew tradition, Job clings to all three of those truths no matter how contradictory they seem.

—Philip Yancey

2. Finally, God swept onto the "stage" of Job's story and, in the last five chapters of the book (Job 38–42), presented his "answer" to Job's questions and accusations.
   a. Describe the theme of God's message and Job's response to his long-awaited, face-to-face encounter with God. (See Job 38:1–3; 40:1–7; 42:1–6.)

God appeared and, rather than letting Job "see behind the curtain," essentially challenged Job on how he thought he knew so much. God showed Job just how limited his human viewpoint was. Job was thoroughly humbled by God's presence and repented of speaking of things he did not (and could not) understand. Job's great challenges suddenly lost their significance when God appeared.

   b. What did God conclude about the arguments of Job's friends? (See Job 42:7–9.)

God said he was angry with Job's friends because, unlike Job, they did not speak the truth about God. God required them to make a sacrifice for their sin.

Please turn to page 47 as we move into the Small Group Exploration part of this session.

Small Group Exploration: A Test of Faith (12 minutes)

Participant's Guide page 47.

The real issue explored in the book of Job is whether a human being will trust a sovereign, invisible God even when circumstances do not support that trust. All of us at times find ourselves in a Job-like state. We may not face disasters of the magnitude of Job's, but we may experience a tragic accident, become terminally ill, or lose a job and begin asking, "Why me? What does God have against me? Why does God seem so distant?"

During such times, we too often view our circumstances as the enemy and center our prayers on our desire for God to change them. Although Job

NOTES

1. Read the following passages from Job 1–2 and note what each reveals about the main characters and plot of the drama that unfolds.
   a. What do we know about Job? (See Job 1:1–5.)
   b. What do we know about Satan, his argument with God, and the results? (See Job 1:6–12; 2:1–7.)
   c. What bad things happened to Job? (See Job 1:13–22; 2:7–10.)
   d. Who came to be with Job, and what was their initial response? (See Job 2:11–13.)

Perspective

Job prefers to live with an agonizing paradox, that God still loves him even though all evidence points against it. His friends laid out the logic: *Suffering comes from God. God is just. Therefore you, Job, are guilty.* After examining his own life, and toying with the notion of an unjust God, Job arrives at a different formula that on the surface makes no sense: *Suffering comes from God. God is just. I am innocent.* In the best Hebrew tradition, Job clings to all three of those truths no matter how contradictory they seem.

—Philip Yancey

2. Finally, God swept onto the "stage" of Job's story and, in the last five chapters of the book (Job 38–42), presented his "answer" to Job's questions and accusations.
   a. Describe the theme of God's message and Job's response to his long-awaited, face-to-face encounter with God. (See Job 38:1–3; 40:1–7; 42:1–6.)
   b. What did God conclude about the arguments of Job's friends? (See Job 42:7–9.)

Small Group Exploration: A Test of Faith

The real issue explored in the book of Job is whether a human being will trust a sovereign, invisible God even when circumstances do not support that trust. All of us at times find ourselves in a Job-like state. We may not face disasters of the magnitude of Job's, but we may experience a tragic accident, become terminally ill, or lose a job and begin asking, "Why me? What does God have against me? Why does God seem so distant?"

During such times, we too often view our circumstances as the enemy and center our prayers on our desire for God to change them. Although Job certainly wanted his miserable circumstances to improve, he also looked beyond those circumstances to his relationship with God. Let's break into groups of three to five and take a closer look to see if Job reveals a different way we can respond to God in the face of our trials.

1. When everything seemed to be stacked against him, what choice did Job's wife urge him to make, and what was his short-term and long-term response? (See Job 2:9–10; 13:15.)

2. Despite their silence upon first seeing Job's plight, Job's three friends—and to a lesser extent a young man named Elihu—had a lot to say. They told Job that a just God treats people fairly and rewards those who obey him. So surely, they reasoned, Job's suffering betrayed some serious, unconfessed sin. For much of the book, they accused and argued their position while Job fought to defend the integrity of his relationship with God.

   Even though Job didn't have the view from "behind the curtain" that we have, he certainly rose to the challenge Satan presented. Read

certainly wanted his miserable circumstances to improve, he also looked beyond those circumstances to his relationship with God. Let's break into groups of three to five and take a closer look to see if Job reveals a different way we can respond to God in the face of our trials.

If you will not be breaking into small groups for the Small Group Exploration, lead the group in a discussion of the following questions.

1. When everything seemed to be stacked against him, what choice did Job's wife urge him to make, and what was his short-term and long-term response? (See Job 2:9–10; 13:15.)

She urged him to curse God and die, but he refused to give up on God even if God were to take his life.

2. Despite their silence upon first seeing Job's plight, Job's three friends—and to a lesser extent a young man named Elihu—had a lot to say. They told Job that a just God treats people fairly and rewards those who obey him. So surely, they reasoned, Job's suffering betrayed some serious, unconfessed sin. For much of the book, they accused and argued their position while Job fought to defend the integrity of his relationship with God.

   Even though Job didn't have the view from "behind the curtain" that we have, he certainly rose to the challenge Satan presented. Read the following passages and note the way Job recognized his human sinfulness, defended his integrity, and clung to God.

Scripture Passage	Job's Response
Job 6:21–29	Job fully recognized his desperate state as well as his friends' fear of his circumstances and condition. He attacked their arguments, questioned their integrity, challenged them to honestly correct his position, and wondered why they treated the words of a despairing man as insignificant.
Job 9:2–20	Job recognized his, and indeed all humankind's, impurity before the holy might and majesty of God.
Job 19:2–27	Job expressed the pain and torment of his friends' sorry comfort. This marvelous speech proclaims his innocence and recognition of what has happened to him and expresses the pain of alienation from family, servants, and friends. Yet Job retained his faith in God—indeed, it was the only hope to which he could cling.
Job 23:2–12	Despite his complaints about his condition, which Job believed came from the hand of God, Job expressed his longing for relationship with God and belief in God's justice and faithfulness.
Job 27:1–8	In this powerful statement about Job's commitment to his faith, he appears to recognize the key question because he asks, "What hope has the godless when he is cut off?" This is the ultimate question of faith: What else is there?

NOTES

Small Group Exploration: A Test of Faith

The real issue explored in the book of Job is whether a human being will trust a sovereign, invisible God even when circumstances do not support that trust. All of us at times find ourselves in a Job-like state. We may not face disasters of the magnitude of Job's, but we may experience a tragic accident, become terminally ill, or lose a job and begin asking, "Why me? What does God have against me? Why does God seem so distant?"

During such times, we too often view our circumstances as the enemy and center our prayers on our desire for God to change them. Although Job certainly wanted his miserable circumstances to improve, he also looked beyond those circumstances to his relationship with God. Let's break into groups of three to five and take a closer look to see if Job reveals a different way we can respond to God in the face of our trials.

1. When everything seemed to be stacked against him, what choice did Job's wife urge him to make, and what was his short-term and long-term response? (See Job 2:9–10; 13:15.)

2. Despite their silence upon first seeing Job's plight, Job's three friends—and to a lesser extent a young man named Elihu—had a lot to say. They told Job that a just God treats people fairly and rewards those who obey him. So surely, they reasoned, Job's suffering betrayed some serious, unconfessed sin. For much of the book, they accused and argued their position while Job fought to defend the integrity of his relationship with God.

   Even though Job didn't have the view from "behind the curtain" that we have, he certainly rose to the challenge Satan presented. Read

   the following passages and note the way Job recognized his human sinfulness, defended his integrity, and clung to God.

Scripture Passage	Job's Response
Job 6:21–29	
Job 9:2–20	
Job 19:2–27	
Job 23:2–12	
Job 27:1–8	

Perspective

Job may have given up on God's justice, but he steadfastly refuses to give up on God. At the most unlikely moments of despair, he comes up with brilliant flashes of hope and faith. . . . Job instinctively believes he is better off casting his lot with God, regardless of how remote or even sadistic God appears at the moment, rather than abandoning all hope.

—Philip Yancey

3. Despite Job's marvelous faith, Philip Yancey has observed that "Job did not take his pain meekly; he cried out in protest to God. His strong remarks scandalized his friends but not God." When we find ourselves in trying circumstances, we may be afraid of somehow insulting God, so we hesitate to express honestly our pain and doubt.

Perspective

Job may have given up on God's justice, but he steadfastly refuses to give up on God. At the most unlikely moments of despair, he comes up with brilliant flashes of hope and faith. . . . Job instinctively believes he is better off casting his lot with God, regardless of how remote or even sadistic God appears at the moment, rather than abandoning all hope.

—Philip Yancey

3. Despite Job's marvelous faith, Philip Yancey has observed that "Job did not take his pain meekly; he cried out in protest to God. His strong remarks scandalized his friends but not God." When we find ourselves in trying circumstances, we may be afraid of somehow insulting God, so we hesitate to express honestly our pain and doubt.

    a. We know from the end of the story that God did not consider Job's honesty to be sin, so consider the following passages and note how strongly Job "let God have it."

Scripture Passage	Job's Accusations
Job 7:17–19; 10:20–21	Job wanted God to "go away" so he could have a little relief, a bit of joy, before he died.
Job 14:18–22	Job was overcome by pain and accused God of wearing away people's hope.
Job 16:7–9	Job was worn out and devastated. He accused God of attacking him, of tearing him, of "gnashing his teeth" at him.

    b. How does this type of expression fit with your picture of what a godly person's relationship with God should look like? What would be your hopes or fears if you dared approach God like this?

Encourage participants to really think about what might happen if they were this passionate and honest with God. Encourage them to express the "pros" and "cons" of a relationship with God that was this genuine.

Perspective

Job faced a crisis of faith, not of suffering. And so do we. All of us at times find ourselves in a Job-like state. . . . At such times we focus too easily on circumstances—illness, our looks, poverty, bad luck—as the enemy. We pray for God to change those circumstances. . . . Job teaches, though, that we need faith most at the precise moment when it seems impossible.

—Philip Yancey

NOTES

the following passages and note the way Job recognized his human sinfulness, defended his integrity, and clung to God.

Scripture Passage	Job's Response
Job 6:21–29	
Job 9:2–20	
Job 19:2–27	
Job 23:2–12	
Job 27:1–8	

Perspective

Job may have given up on God's justice, but he steadfastly refuses to give up on God. At the most unlikely moments of despair, he comes up with brilliant flashes of hope and faith. . . . Job instinctively believes he is better off casting his lot with God, regardless of how remote or even sadistic God appears at the moment, rather than abandoning all hope.

—Philip Yancey

3. Despite Job's marvelous faith, Philip Yancey has observed that "Job did not take his pain meekly; he cried out in protest to God. His strong remarks scandalized his friends but not God." When we find ourselves in trying circumstances, we may be afraid of somehow insulting God, so we hesitate to express honestly our pain and doubt.

a. We know from the end of the story that God did not consider Job's honesty to be sin, so consider the following passages and note how strongly Job "let God have it."

Scripture Passage	Job's Accusations
Job 7:17–19; 10:20–21	
Job 14:18–22	
Job 16:7–9	

b. How does this type of expression fit with your picture of what a godly person's relationship with God should look like? What would be your hopes or fears if you dared approach God like this?

Perspective

Job faced a crisis of faith, not of suffering. And so do we. All of us at times find ourselves in a Job-like state. . . . At such times we focus too easily on circumstances—illness, our looks, poverty, bad luck—as the enemy. We pray for God to change those circumstances. . . . Job teaches, though, that we need faith most at the precise moment when it seems impossible.

—Philip Yancey

If you have divided into small groups, let participants know when there is 1 minute remaining.

Give participants a moment to transition from their small group discussions. If time allows, or if you have assigned each group a specific question, have representatives from the groups share their key ideas.

Now let's wrap up our Group Discovery time. Please turn to page 50.

Group Discussion (5 minutes)

Participant's Guide page 50.

Use one or more of the following questions to encourage participants to share their observations with the entire group.

One Person's Choice Makes a Difference

C. S. Lewis said, "There is no neutral ground in the universe: every square inch, every split second, is claimed by God and counterclaimed by Satan." ... Job presents the astounding truth that our choices of faith matter not just to us and our own destiny but, amazingly, to God himself.... How we respond *matters*. By hanging onto the thinnest thread of faith, Job won a crucial victory in God's grand plan to redeem the earth. In his grace, God has given ordinary men and women the dignity of participating in the redemption of the cosmos.

—Philip Yancey

1. Job's story showed Philip Yancey that "a piece of the history of the universe was at stake in Job, and is still at stake in our own responses," so our choices of faith and our prayers of faith matter to God.

   a. In what ways do you agree or disagree with this statement?

   b. In what ways do you find this hard to believe about yourself?

   c. Can you think of other portions of Scripture that indicate this truth?

Note: If no one can think of any passages, you might suggest they consider Daniel 10:10–14 or Luke 10:17–19. If participants need additional input, refer to the box "One Person's Choice Makes a Difference."

Perspective

We will never know, in this life, the full significance of our actions here for, as Job demonstrates, much takes place invisible to us. Jesus' cross offers a pattern for that too: what seemed very ordinary, one more dreary feat of colonial "justice" in a Roman outpost, made possible the salvation of the entire world.

—Philip Yancey

NOTES

Group Discussion

One Person's Choice Makes a Difference

C. S. Lewis said, "There is no neutral ground in the universe: every square inch, every split second, is claimed by God and counterclaimed by Satan." ... Job presents the astounding truth that our choices of faith matter not just to us and our own destiny but, amazingly, to God himself.... How we respond *matters*. By hanging onto the thinnest thread of faith, Job won a crucial victory in God's grand plan to redeem the earth. In his grace, God has given ordinary men and women the dignity of participating in the redemption of the cosmos.

—Philip Yancey

1. Job's story showed Philip Yancey that "a piece of the history of the universe was at stake in Job, and is still at stake in our own responses," so our choices of faith and our prayers of faith matter to God.
   a. In what ways do you agree or disagree with this statement?
   b. In what ways do you find this hard to believe about yourself?
   c. Can you think of other portions of Scripture that indicate this truth?

Perspective

We will never know, in this life, the full significance of our actions here for, as Job demonstrates, much takes place invisible to us. Jesus' cross offers a pattern for that too: what seemed very ordinary, one more dreary feat of colonial "justice" in a Roman outpost, made possible the salvation of the entire world.

—Philip Yancey

2. At the end of the book of Job, God criticized Job for just one thing: his limited point of view.
   a. In what ways is God's criticism of Job true of us as well?
   b. Why is it so tempting to make judgments about God based on incomplete evidence?

Why Suffering?

The Bible gives many examples of suffering that, like Job's, have nothing to do with God's punishment. In all his miracles of healing, Jesus overturned the notion, widespread at the time, that suffering—blindness, lameness, leprosy—comes to people who deserve it. Jesus grieved over many things that happen on this planet, a sure sign that God regrets them far more than we do.... The Bible supplies no systematic answers to the "Why?" questions ... we dare not tread into areas God has sealed off as his domain. Divine providence is a mystery that only God understands, and belongs in what I have called "The Encyclopedia of Theological Ignorance" for a simple reason: no time-bound human, living on a rebellious planet, blind to the realities of the unseen world, has the ability to comprehend such answers—God's reply to Job in a nutshell.

—Philip Yancey

2. At the end of the book of Job, God criticized Job for just one thing: his limited point of view.

    a. In what ways is God's criticism of Job true of us as well?

    b. Why is it so tempting to make judgments about God based on incomplete evidence?

Why Suffering?

The Bible gives many examples of suffering that, like Job's, have nothing to do with God's punishment. In all his miracles of healing, Jesus overturned the notion, widespread at the time, that suffering—blindness, lameness, leprosy—comes to people who deserve it. Jesus grieved over many things that happen on this planet, a sure sign that God regrets them far more than we do. . . . The Bible supplies no systematic answers to the "Why?" questions . . . we dare not tread into areas God has sealed off as his domain. Divine providence is a mystery that only God understands, and belongs in what I have called "The Encyclopedia of Theological Ignorance" for a simple reason: no time-bound human, living on a rebellious planet, blind to the realities of the unseen world, has the ability to comprehend such answers—God's reply to Job in a nutshell.

—Philip Yancey

3. The book of Job shows us that God cares deeply about not only how we respond to our distress but how we respond to him when we face distress.

    a. Did you realize that we bring God great pleasure when we honestly put our faith in him?

    b. How does it feel to know that God actually takes delight in his relationship with you?

Now it's time for each of us to consider on a personal level what we've been discussing and thinking about. Please turn to page 53.

5 min. PERSONAL JOURNEY: TO BEGIN NOW

Participant's Guide page 53.

The story of Job is a drama of cosmic proportions presented through the context of suffering. The theme of suffering is woven into the fabric of the story, but the story of Job isn't actually about undeserved suffering. It is about having faith in God when faith seems impossible.

NOTES

Perspective

We will never know, in this life, the full significance of our actions here for, as Job demonstrates, much takes place invisible to us. Jesus' cross offers a pattern for that too: what seemed very ordinary, one more dreary feat of colonial "justice" in a Roman outpost, made possible the salvation of the entire world.

—Philip Yancey

2. At the end of the book of Job, God criticized Job for just one thing: his limited point of view.
   a. In what ways is God's criticism of Job true of us as well?
   b. Why is it so tempting to make judgments about God based on incomplete evidence?

Why Suffering?

The Bible gives many examples of suffering that, like Job's, have nothing to do with God's punishment. In all his miracles of healing, Jesus overturned the notion, widespread at the time, that suffering—blindness, lameness, leprosy—comes to people who deserve it. Jesus grieved over many things that happen on this planet, a sure sign that God regrets them far more than we do. . . . The Bible supplies no systematic answers to the "Why?" questions . . . we dare not tread into areas God has sealed off as his domain. Divine providence is a mystery that only God understands, and belongs in what I have called "The Encyclopedia of Theological Ignorance" for a simple reason: no time-bound human, living on a rebellious planet, blind to the realities of the unseen world, has the ability to comprehend such answers—God's reply to Job in a nutshell.

—Philip Yancey

3. The book of Job shows us that God cares deeply about not only how we respond to our distress but how we respond to him when we face distress.
   a. Did you realize that we bring God great pleasure when we honestly put our faith in him?
   b. How does it feel to know that God actually takes delight in his relationship with you?

Personal Journey: To Begin Now

The story of Job is a drama of cosmic proportions presented through the context of suffering. The theme of suffering is woven into the fabric of the story, but the story of Job isn't actually about undeserved suffering. It is about having faith in God when faith seems impossible. Take some time now by yourself to consider what you have discovered in this session and how it applies to your daily life.

1. Identify your battleground of faith–career failure, floundering marriage, ill health–the area of life that makes faith in God seem impossible at times. In what ways have you based your faith on who God is, and in what ways have you based it on what he provides?
2. The big question of Job's drama isn't *why* we suffer, but *how* we respond to suffering. The "behind the curtain" glimpse of Job's ordeal that the Bible gives us reveals that in God's plan suffering can serve a higher good. Just as God allowed Job's suffering to occur in order to refute Satan's challenge (which called into question the entire human experiment), God continues to use suffering in ways we may not be able to see or understand.
   a. When the facts don't add up and you see the face of unexplained suffering, how do you typically respond to God?

Take some time now by yourself to consider what you have discovered in this session and how it applies to your daily life.

1. Identify your battleground of faith—career failure, floundering marriage, ill health—the area of life that makes faith in God seem impossible at times. In what ways have you based your faith on who God is, and in what ways have you based it on what he provides?

2. The big question of Job's drama isn't *why* we suffer, but *how* we respond to suffering. The "behind the curtain" glimpse of Job's ordeal that the Bible gives us reveals that in God's plan suffering can serve a higher good. Just as God allowed Job's suffering to occur in order to refute Satan's challenge (which called into question the entire human experiment), God continues to use suffering in ways we may not be able to see or understand.

   a. When the facts don't add up and you see the face of unexplained suffering, how do you typically respond to God?

   b. If God audibly spoke to you about how you've responded to him during difficult times, what might he say? You might want to keep his evaluation of Job and his friends (Job 42:7–9) in mind.

   c. How would you want God's response to be different?

   d. If you believe that God can indeed use suffering for your good—and the good of other people—what impact does that belief have on your life?

3. The book of Job affirms that God hears our cries and is in control of this world no matter how bad things may appear to be. God did not answer all of Job's questions, but in God's presence Job's doubts melted away, and that was enough.

   a. When Job came face to face with God, Job saw God in a way he never had before. It seemed to be enough that God ruled the universe and loved him. Is that enough for you? What are the implications of your answer?

   b. What are your honest feelings about the statement that God cares more about your response to him than he does about your pleasure? Do you think God can "handle" those feelings? How do those feelings affect your relationship with God?

Perspective

When a Job-like circumstance happens to you, I guarantee you that someone has been there before you. And that's the old man Job. Because he was honest, because he was so eloquent, he's like a pioneer. He has gone ahead of us. So if you wonder, *Should I really feel that? Should I really say that to God?* you can relax and say, "Well, yeah, that's okay because Job already did."

—Philip Yancey

NOTES

Personal Journey: To Begin Now

The story of Job is a drama of cosmic proportions presented through the context of suffering. The theme of suffering is woven into the fabric of the story, but the story of Job isn't actually about undeserved suffering. It is about having faith in God when faith seems impossible. Take some time now by yourself to consider what you have discovered in this session and how it applies to your daily life.

1. Identify your battleground of faith—career failure, floundering marriage, ill health—the area of life that makes faith in God seem impossible at times. In what ways have you based your faith on who God is, and in what ways have you based it on what he provides?

2. The big question of Job's drama isn't *why* we suffer, but *how* we respond to suffering. The "behind the curtain" glimpse of Job's ordeal that the Bible gives us reveals that in God's plan suffering can serve a higher good. Just as God allowed Job's suffering to occur in order to refute Satan's challenge (which called into question the entire human experiment), God continues to use suffering in ways we may not be able to see or understand.

   a. When the facts don't add up and you see the face of unexplained suffering, how do you typically respond to God?

   b. If God audibly spoke to you about how you've responded to him during difficult times, what might he say? You might want to keep his evaluation of Job and his friends (Job 42:7–9) in mind.

   c. How would you want God's response to be different?

   d. If you believe that God can indeed use suffering for your good—and the good of other people—what impact does that belief have on your life?

3. The book of Job affirms that God hears our cries and is in control of this world no matter how bad things may appear to be. God did not answer all of Job's questions, but in God's presence Job's doubts melted away, and that was enough.

   a. When Job came face to face with God, Job saw God in a way he never had before. It seemed to be enough that God ruled the universe and loved him. Is that enough for you? What are the implications of your answer?

   b. What are your honest feelings about the statement that God cares more about your response to him than he does about your pleasure? Do you think God can "handle" those feelings? How do those feelings affect your relationship with God?

Perspective

When a Job-like circumstance happens to you, I guarantee you that someone has been there before you. And that's the old man Job. Because he was honest, because he was so eloquent, he's like a pioneer. He has gone ahead of us. So if you wonder, *Should I really feel that? Should I really say that to God?* you can relax and say, "Well, yeah, that's okay because Job already did."

—Philip Yancey

Let participants know when there is 1 minute remaining. Remind participants that they may want to continue their journey by completing the additional exercise on page 56 of their Participant's Guide before the next session.

PERSONAL JOURNEY: TO DO BETWEEN SESSIONS

Before the next session, set aside time away from distractions to ask God to draw you closer to him.

1. Seek to deepen your relationship with God so that you can respond in faith when you face challenges that make faith seem impossible. The passages below will help remind you of God's care for those who turn to him in their distress. Read and meditate on each one and write a short journal entry focusing on how deeply God cares for his suffering servants.

Scripture Passage	God's Care for Those Who Trust Him
Psalm 9:9–10	
Psalm 33:12–19	
Psalm 34:15–22	
Isaiah 46:9–11	
Isaiah 49:13–16	
Nahum 1:7	

2. Some of God's most righteous and faithful people have had to endure great trials. In Ezekiel 14:14, God mentions Job, Daniel, and Noah. We have focused on Job's story in this session, but you may also want to read about Daniel's trial (Daniel 6) and Noah's trial (Genesis 6:5–22; 7:13–18; 8).

1 min. CLOSING MEDITATION

Let's take a moment to close in prayer.

Dear God, sometimes it seems as if life is simply too tough to endure, but you want us, above all, to place our faith in you. Help us to commit our ways to you and to keep trusting in you. Help us to be still before you and wait patiently for you to act. How much we need your peace! As we face suffering, keep us from stumbling. We are so grateful that you will not forsake your faithful people. We wait for that wonderful day when you will reward us for our faith for all eternity. Amen.

—Prayer inspired by Psalm 37

NOTES

Personal Journey: To Do between Sessions

Before the next session, set aside time away from distractions to ask God to draw you closer to him.

1. Seek to deepen your relationship with God so that you can respond in faith when you face challenges that make faith seem impossible. The passages below will help remind you of God's care for those who turn to him in their distress. Read and meditate on each one and write a short journal entry focusing on how deeply God cares for his suffering servants.

Scripture Passage	God's Care for Those Who Trust Him
Psalm 9:9–10	
Psalm 33:12–19	
Psalm 34:15–22	
Isaiah 46:9–11	
Isaiah 49:13–16	
Nahum 1:7	

2. Some of God's most righteous and faithful people have had to endure great trials. In Ezekiel 14:14, God mentions Job, Daniel, and Noah. We have focused on Job's story in this session, but you may also want to read about Daniel's trial (Daniel 6) and Noah's trial (Genesis 6:5–22; 7:13–18; 8).

SESSION FOUR

Deuteronomy: A Taste of Bittersweet

BEFORE YOU LEAD

Synopsis

In this session we encounter Moses, one of the greatest figures in the Old Testament. Although many of us know some highlights of Moses' life—his rescue from the Nile, his princely upbringing, his murderous rage and self-imposed exile, his calling by God to confront Pharaoh and lead the Hebrews out of Egypt, his receipt of the Ten Commandments, his leadership during the desert wanderings—few of us take much note of the end of Moses' life. The book of Deuteronomy is an account of Moses' parting words to the Hebrews.

By this time Moses is old and weary, his life nearly over. Only Moses, Joshua, and Caleb remember the enslavement in Egypt firsthand. The Hebrews are about to fulfill their dream of crossing the Jordan River and marching into God's Promised Land. But Moses will not be a part of it; he must stay behind while the others press on. He has one last chance to prepare the people for what lies ahead.

The book of Deuteronomy recounts not only the Hebrews' remarkable transformation in the desert but Moses' transformation as well. By God's power and grace, the Hebrew slaves, whose hearts were tied to Egypt, were transformed into a new generation eager to possess their God-given land. By the power of God's hand, Moses was transformed from a stuttering shepherd with the blood of a Hebrew and the training of an Egyptian prince into one of the greatest (if not *the* greatest) leaders in human history. Deuteronomy is Moses' valedictory speech—explaining to the Hebrews what had gone before, understanding what was at stake in the present, and warning of what would come.

Throughout Deuteronomy, Moses emphasized one theme: *God* did it. *God* saved him from death as an infant and gave him a superb education. While Moses tended sheep, learned desert survival skills, and raised a family, *God* listened to the groans of the Hebrew slaves. *God* then chose Moses—a hot-headed murderer who had tried single-handedly to help the Hebrews—to be the first intermediary between God and his people. *God* enabled Moses to present God's demands to the mighty Pharaoh. *God* sent the plagues that caused Pharaoh to send the Hebrews (laden with Egypt's wealth) packing. *God* provided food, water, and direction during the journey to the Promised Land. In fact, God even designated the Exodus as a way of describing himself: "I am the LORD your God, who brought you out of Egypt" (Deuteronomy 5:6).

Not surprisingly, Moses dedicated much of his speech to urging the Hebrews to remember. He reminded them that success, not failure, is the greatest danger facing any follower of God. He reminded them that God is a living person, not a silent, impersonal, manmade god like those of the Egyptians or Canaanites. He reminded them where they had come from and where God wanted to take them. He reminded them that they were God's "peculiar people," chosen by God to be different from any other nation.

Shortly before he died and the Hebrews entered the Promised Land, Moses made them learn their history. They needed to remember everything that had happened so that they would not take credit for their successes and forget about God. So he taught them the Song of Moses, which was really a history lesson, and they sang it as they marched into the Promised Land. In this session we, too, will be challenged to remember what God has done for us in the past so that we will live as "his people" from now on.

Key Points of This Session

1. Deuteronomy records Moses' parting words as the Hebrews stood ready to cross the Jordan River and possess the Promised Land. Success—the land of milk and honey—was at last within their grasp, and Moses saw trouble ahead. He had learned that success is dangerous, so in the strongest terms, he warned them to be careful.
2. Over and over again, Moses commanded the people not to forget about God. The tired old man who talked with God challenged them to remember what God had done for them. He reminded them that God had chosen them to be his holy people. He urged them to remember where they had been so they could go forward to where they were destined to go.

Suggested Reading

This session corresponds to Chapter 3 of *The Bible Jesus Read*. You may want to read this chapter in order to deepen your understanding of this material.

Session Outline (52 minutes)

I. Introduction (5 minutes)
  A. Welcome
  B. What's to Come
  C. Questions to Think About
II. Video Presentation: "Deuteronomy: A Taste of Bittersweet" (11 minutes)
III. Group Discovery (30 minutes)
  A. Video Highlights (5 minutes)
  B. Large Group Exploration: Get Ready ... Get Set ... Remember! (10 minutes)
  C. Small Group Exploration: A Peculiar People (10 minutes)
  D. Group Discussion (5 minutes)
IV. Personal Journey (5 minutes)
V. Closing Meditation (1 minute)

Materials

You'll need a VCR, TV, and Bible. You may also find a whiteboard, flip chart, or overhead projector to be a useful tool in guiding group discussion. View the video prior to leading the session so you are familiar with its main points.

SESSION FOUR

Deuteronomy: A Taste of Bittersweet

> Like a parent trying to teach an unruly bunch of children how to behave as adults . . . Moses had one last shot, one last opportunity to pass along historical memory, to purge himself of grievances and pain, to bequeath to them the hope and grit they would desperately need in his absence.
>
> —Philip Yancey

5 min. INTRODUCTION

Welcome

Welcome participants to Session 4 of *The Bible Jesus Read* course: "Deuteronomy: A Taste of Bittersweet."

What's to Come

In this session we encounter Moses, one of the greatest figures in the Old Testament. Although many of us know some highlights of Moses' life, few of us take much note of the end of his life. The book of Deuteronomy is an account of Moses' farewell speech to the Hebrews.

By this time, Moses is old and weary. The Hebrews' dream of crossing the Jordan River and marching into God's Promised Land is about to be fulfilled, but Moses knows he will not be a part of it. So this is his last chance to prepare God's people for what lies ahead. We'll pay particular attention to Moses' warnings and to the importance of remembering what God has done, and is doing, in the lives of his people.

Let's begin by considering a few questions. Please turn to page 57 of your Participant's Guide.

Questions to Think About

Participant's Guide page 57.

As time permits, ask two or more of the following questions and solicit responses from the participants.

NOTES

SESSION FOUR

Deuteronomy: A Taste of Bittersweet

> Like a parent trying to teach an unruly bunch of children how to behave as adults . . . Moses had one last shot, one last opportunity to pass along historical memory, to purge himself of grievances and pain, to bequeath to them the hope and grit they would desperately need in his absence.
>
> —Philip Yancey

Questions to Think About

1. What do you know about the book of Deuteronomy? What do you think God's purpose was in preserving its message for us?

2. Would you say you are more attentive and obedient to God when things in your life are going well or when you are facing difficulties? Explain your answer and share some examples from your life.

3. Most of us would say that we remember the basics of our faith. We would claim to remember the important stories in Scripture and to remember what God teaches us. But how well do we *really* remember what God says? Let's take a few moments to name as many of the Ten Commandments as we can.

1. What do you know about the book of Deuteronomy? What do you think God's purpose was in preserving its message for us?

Responses may vary. The intent of this question is to take inventory of what your group understands of this often neglected book. Some may have no understanding of it, which is a good reason to study it!

2. Would you say you are more attentive and obedient to God when things in your life are going well or when you are facing difficulties? Explain your answer and share some examples from your life.

Again, this is a "taking inventory" type of question. The intent is not to arrive at a "right" or "wrong" answer, but to raise a question that will be explored more fully in this session.

3. Most of us would say that we remember the basics of our faith. We would claim to remember the important stories in Scripture and to remember what God teaches us. But how well do we *really* remember what God says? Let's take a few moments to name as many of the Ten Commandments as we can.

Most people will be able to name only three or four of the Ten Commandments. This question is a bit of a wake-up call to help participants realize how easily we forget what God teaches us.

Note: If you need help, the Ten Commandments are found in Deuteronomy 5:1–22.

Let's keep these ideas in mind as we view the video. There is space to take notes on page 58.

11 min. VIDEO PRESENTATION: "DEUTERONOMY: A TASTE OF BITTERSWEET"

Participant's Guide page 58.

Leader's Video Observations

A perspective on history

NOTES

SESSION FOUR

Deuteronomy: A Taste of Bittersweet

> Like a parent trying to teach an unruly bunch of children how to behave as adults . . . Moses had one last shot, one last opportunity to pass along historical memory, to purge himself of grievances and pain, to bequeath to them the hope and grit they would desperately need in his absence.
>
> —Philip Yancey

Questions to Think About

1. What do you know about the book of Deuteronomy? What do you think God's purpose was in preserving its message for us?

2. Would you say you are more attentive and obedient to God when things in your life are going well or when you are facing difficulties? Explain your answer and share some examples from your life.

3. Most of us would say that we remember the basics of our faith. We would claim to remember the important stories in Scripture and to remember what God teaches us. But how well do we *really* remember what God says? Let's take a few moments to name as many of the Ten Commandments as we can.

Video Presentation: "Deuteronomy: A Taste of Bittersweet"

A perspective on history

Moses speaks

Things are looking up. Don't blow it!

Remember where you came from

God chooses a people to create a culture

Deuteronomy for our time

Moses speaks

Things are looking up. Don't blow it!

Remember where you came from

God chooses a people to create a culture

Deuteronomy for our time

30 min. GROUP DISCOVERY

If your group has seven or more members, use the Video Highlights with the entire group (5 minutes), then complete the Large Group Exploration (10 minutes), and then break into small groups of three to five people for the Small Group Exploration (10 minutes). Finally, bring everyone together for the closing Group Discussion (5 minutes).

If your group has fewer than seven members, begin with the Video Highlights (5 minutes), then complete both the Large Group Exploration (10 minutes) and the Small Group Exploration (10 minutes) as a group. Wrap up your discovery time with the Group Discussion (5 minutes).

Please turn to page 59 as we discuss some questions related to the video segment we have just seen.

Video Highlights (5 minutes)

Participant's Guide page 59.

As time permits, ask one or more of the following questions, which directly relate to the video the participants have just seen.

NOTES

Video Presentation: "Deuteronomy: A Taste of Bittersweet"

A perspective on history

Moses speaks

Things are looking up. Don't blow it!

Remember where you came from

God chooses a people to create a culture

Deuteronomy for our time

1. At the beginning, Philip said, "When things are really going well, that's when you are in danger. Look out. Watch out." Explain why it's easier to forget about God when things are going well. What biblical or contemporary examples of this principle come to mind?

Most participants will realize that when things are going well it's easy to take credit for our success and forget about God. One standout example would be Solomon, who "had it all" and forgot about God, producing disastrous results. More contemporary examples would be former president Bill Clinton or other famous leaders who have "messed up." Encourage participants to begin thinking about the truth of this statement in their own lives as well.

2. Moses had spent more than a generation leading the Hebrews to the Promised Land. He had known them when they suffered as slaves in Egypt. For more than forty years he had seen them at their best and at their worst. He had listened, coaxed, scolded, fasted, taught, suffered, prayed, judged, mediated, and so much more—all on their behalf.

   a. What do you think Moses must have felt as he stood before that vast throng and prepared to speak to them for the last time?

Encourage participants to consider what it would be like to have walked in Moses' shoes. "Bittersweet" is probably a good description: incredible hope balanced by a sense of desperation that they at last "get it right"; a sense of triumph tempered by fear that he has missed something in their preparation; incredible joy that the goal is so close countered by deep regret that he can go no farther, etc. We might experience similar feelings when we send a child off to college.

   b. Why do you think Moses thought it was so important to teach the Hebrews' history to this new generation? If you had been Moses, what do you think you would have been compelled to tell them before you died?

Responses will vary but may include: Moses obviously didn't want the new generation to have to endure the same pitfalls as their parents, and he wanted God's plan to succeed. If they forgot what God had already done for them, they might not realize how much God valued being in relationship with them. If they knew the sins for which God had punished their parents, they might not commit the same ones. If they remembered what God had already done for them, they might have hope when things became difficult.

Now we're ready for the Large Group Exploration part of this session. Please turn to page 61.

NOTES

Video Highlights

1. At the beginning, Philip said, "When things are really going well, that's when you are in danger. Look out. Watch out." Explain why it's easier to forget about God when things are going well. What biblical or contemporary examples of this principle come to mind?

2. Moses had spent more than a generation leading the Hebrews to the Promised Land. He had known them when they suffered as slaves in Egypt. For more than forty years he had seen them at their best and at their worst. He had listened, coaxed, scolded, fasted, taught, suffered, prayed, judged, mediated, and so much more—all on their behalf.

   a. What do you think Moses must have felt as he stood before that vast throng and prepared to speak to them for the last time?

   b. Why do you think Moses thought it was so important to teach the Hebrews' history to this new generation? If you had been Moses, what do you think you would have been compelled to tell them before you died?

Did You Know?

Nothing, apparently, bothers God more than the simple act of being forgotten. . . . On the first day they [the Israelites] ate produce from the Promised Land, the manna would stop. From then on they must cultivate their own land and plant their own crops. They would build cities, fight wars, appoint a king. They would prosper and grow plump. They would trust their armies and chariots instead of their God, forgetting the lesson inflicted on almighty Egypt. They would discriminate against the poor and the aliens, forgetting they were once both. In a word, they would forget God.

—Philip Yancey

Large Group Exploration: Get Ready . . . Get Set . . . Remember! (10 minutes)

Participant's Guide page 61.

Read the introductory paragraphs to the group, then begin discussing the questions that follow.

In the video, Philip Yancey said, "Moses was saying, 'You are ready now. Don't blow it. . . . This is a new generation. It's a new world, and I want you to go into this land with hope and promise and confidence that your parents who had started off as slaves in Egypt never felt.'"

Moses took definite steps to encourage the people to focus their minds and hearts on God as they entered the Promised Land. Let's look at some of those steps and consider how they apply to our lives today.

1. God had specific requirements for his people to obey so that they could reap all of the blessings of the land he had promised. What did Moses tell the people to do in order to impress upon them the importance of their obedience? (See Deuteronomy 6:1–9; 11:18–21.)

He told them to love God and allow the commandments to enter their hearts and minds—to permeate their whole being; to impress the commandments on their children, reinforcing the truth all through the day during various activities; to tie symbols on their hands and to wear symbols on their foreheads; to write the commandments on their doorframes and gates. In short, he told them to surround themselves with God's commandments so that everywhere they went they would be reminded of them and would obey.

2. Which annual celebration did Moses establish, and why? (See Deuteronomy 16:1–8.)

NOTES

Did You Know?

Nothing, apparently, bothers God more than the simple act of being forgotten. . . . On the first day they [the Israelites] ate produce from the Promised Land, the manna would stop. From then on they must cultivate their own land and plant their own crops. They would build cities, fight wars, appoint a king. They would prosper and grow plump. They would trust their armies and chariots instead of their God, forgetting the lesson inflicted on almighty Egypt. They would discriminate against the poor and the aliens, forgetting they were once both. In a word, they would forget God.

—Philip Yancey

Large Group Exploration: Get Ready . . . Get Set . . . Remember!

In the video, Philip Yancey said, "Moses was saying, 'You are ready now. Don't blow it. . . . This is a new generation. It's a new world, and I want you to go into this land with hope and promise and confidence that your parents who had started off as slaves in Egypt never felt.'"

Moses took definite steps to encourage the people to focus their minds and hearts on God as they entered the Promised Land. Let's look at some of those steps and consider how they apply to our lives today.

1. God had specific requirements for his people to obey so that they could reap all of the blessings of the land he had promised. What did Moses tell the people to do in order to impress upon them the importance of their obedience? (See Deuteronomy 6:1–9; 11:18–21.)

2. Which annual celebration did Moses establish, and why? (See Deuteronomy 16:1–8.)

He established the Passover celebration as a remembrance of what God had done in delivering the Hebrews from Egypt. The people were to sacrifice at a specific time and in a specific place, they were not to eat specific foods, and they were to follow through with other specific Passover activities, all of which were reminders of what God had done for them.

3. What did Moses and the elders command the people to do as soon as they crossed the Jordan River and entered the Promised Land? Why do you think they commanded this? (See Deuteronomy 27:1–8.)

Moses and the elders told the Hebrews to set up large stones on Mount Ebal, to coat them with plaster, and to write the words of the law on them. The people were also to build an altar of stones and to make offerings. Through these actions, they were establishing a monument to what God had done and would do for them. These "standing stones" would be a monument to God and his laws and would help the people remember.

4. Even though Moses had already commanded the people to remember and obey God in the activities of daily life, through a celebratory feast and by the building of monuments, he provided them with more reminders.

   a. What else did Moses command the people to do, and why? (See Deuteronomy 27:11–26.)

Moses commanded the twelve tribes to form two choirs—one to bless the people, one to pronounce curses—after they crossed the Jordan River. The people entering the Promised Land would pass between the choirs and hear the obvious differences between what each choir was singing. It was another way for the children of Israel to remember and understand the importance of obeying God.

   b. What other musical memorial did God command Moses to write? What was its purpose? (See Deuteronomy 31:19–22.)

The Song of Moses was a warning of what would happen if the Hebrews did not obey God. The people were to sing it as they marched into the Promised Land. They needed to be aware of the dangers ahead and to remember that God was watching.

Perspective

During the years of wilderness wanderings, forced to depend on God daily, the Hebrews did not have the luxury of forgetting. God fed the Israelites, clothed them, planned their daily itinerary, and fought their battles. No Hebrew questioned the existence of God in those days, for he hovered before them in a thick cloud and a pillar of fire.

—Philip Yancey

NOTES

3. What did Moses and the elders command the people to do as soon as they crossed the Jordan River and entered the Promised Land? Why do you think they commanded this? (See Deuteronomy 27:1–8.)

4. Even though Moses had already commanded the people to remember and obey God in the activities of daily life, through a celebratory feast and by the building of monuments, he provided additional reminders.

   a. What else did Moses command the people to do, and why? (See Deuteronomy 27:11–26.)

   b. What other musical memorial did God command Moses to write? What was its purpose? (See Deuteronomy 31:19–22.)

Perspective

During the years of wilderness wanderings, forced to depend on God daily, the Hebrews did not have the luxury of forgetting. God fed the Israelites, clothed them, planned their daily itinerary, and fought their battles. No Hebrew questioned the existence of God in those days, for he hovered before them in a thick cloud and a pillar of fire.

—Philip Yancey

5. Deuteronomy 8 could be viewed as a representative summary of the book of Deuteronomy. What is the recurring theme of this chapter?

Deuteronomy 8	Theme
vv. 1–2	
vv. 10–14	
vv. 17–18	
vv. 19–20	

5. Deuteronomy 8 could be viewed as a representative summary of the book of Deuteronomy. What is the recurring theme of this chapter?

Deuteronomy 8	Theme
vv. 1–2	Remember what God has done for you
vv. 10–14	When things go well, don't forget
vv. 17–18	Remember, your ability to produce wealth comes from God
vv. 19–20	If you forget God, you will be destroyed

Remember to Remember

God wanted his people to remember their history so that they would not forget to obey him. The verses below highlight just a few of the truths and events God wanted his people to remember. Consider each truth or event and the impact that memory could have on one's relationship with God.

Verses in Deuteronomy	What the Israelites Were to Remember
4:10–12	The day they stood before the Lord at Horeb and heard his words from the fire
5:15	How God miraculously removed them from slavery in Egypt
7:18–19	What God did to Pharaoh and all Egypt
8:2–4	How God had led them and cared for them in the desert for forty years
8:18	The God who gave them the ability to produce wealth and so confirmed his covenant with them
9:7–14	How their repeated sin so provoked God that he wanted to destroy them
24:17–22	That they were once slaves in Egypt, so they were to care for the alien, the fatherless, and the widowed

Please turn to page 65 as we move into the Small Group Exploration part of this session.

Small Group Exploration: A Peculiar People (10 minutes)

Participant's Guide page 65.

During the video presentation, Philip spoke about God calling the Hebrews "my peculiar people." They were to be different from any other nation. They were to think differently. They were to act differently. They were, in a nutshell, to be God's *holy* people, God's "set apart" people who would show others what God is like. Let's break into groups of three to five and take a look at a few passages in Deuteronomy that will help us

NOTES

Perspective

During the years of wilderness wanderings, forced to depend on God daily, the Hebrews did not have the luxury of forgetting. God fed the Israelites, clothed them, planned their daily itinerary, and fought their battles. No Hebrew questioned the existence of God in those days, for he hovered before them in a thick cloud and a pillar of fire.

—Philip Yancey

5. Deuteronomy 8 could be viewed as a representative summary of the book of Deuteronomy. What is the recurring theme of this chapter?

Deuteronomy 8	Theme
vv. 1–2	
vv. 10–14	
vv. 17–18	
vv. 19–20	

Remember to Remember

God wanted his people to remember their history so that they would not forget to obey him. The verses below highlight just a few of the truths and events God wanted his people to remember. Consider each truth or event and the impact that memory could have on one's relationship with God.

Verses in Deuteronomy	What the Israelites Were to Remember
4:10–12	The day they stood before the Lord at Horeb and heard his words from the fire
5:15	How God miraculously removed them from slavery in Egypt
7:18–19	What God did to Pharaoh and all Egypt
8:2–4	How God had led them and cared for them in the desert for forty years
8:18	The God who gave them the ability to produce wealth and so confirmed his covenant with them
9:7–14	How their repeated sin so provoked God that he wanted to destroy them
24:17–22	That they were once slaves in Egypt, so they were to care for the alien, the fatherless, and the widowed

Small Group Exploration: A Peculiar People

During the video presentation, Philip spoke about God calling the Hebrews "my peculiar people." They were to be different from any other nation. They were to think differently. They were to act differently. They were, in a nutshell, to be God's *holy* people, God's "set apart" people who would show others what God is like. Let's break into groups of three to five and take a look at a few passages in Deuteronomy that will help us understand what God had in mind for the people who would represent him to the world.

1. What was unique about the Hebrews? (See Deuteronomy 7:6–9.)

2. In Deuteronomy 7:12–14, we see how serious God considers his covenant to be. What did the Hebrews have to do in order to receive the benefits of God's covenant with them?

3. After Moses reviewed all the terms of God's covenant to the people, note what Moses emphasized. (See Deuteronomy 26:16–19.)

   a. What were the people to do (v. 16)?

understand what God had in mind for the people who would represent him to the world.

If you will not be breaking into small groups for the Small Group Exploration, lead the group in a discussion of the following questions.

1. What was unique about the Hebrews? (See Deuteronomy 7:6–9.)

God had chosen them to be his people, he loved them, he delivered them from Egypt because of the promises he had made to Abraham generations earlier, and he would keep his promises for a thousand generations if they would be faithful to him.

2. In Deuteronomy 7:12–14, we see how serious God considers his covenant to be. What did the Hebrews have to do in order to receive the benefits of God's covenant with them?

God takes his covenants very seriously, so the Hebrews needed to take their covenant with him seriously as well. If they would love God, learn his laws, and keep his commands, God promised to love them, bless them, increase their numbers, keep them healthy, win their battles, bless their children, give them good weather, and bless their crops and animals. In short, God promised to bless the Hebrews more than any other people.

3. After Moses reviewed all the terms of God's covenant to the people, note what Moses emphasized. (See Deuteronomy 26:16–19.)

   a. What were the people to do (v. 16)?

They were to follow God's laws with all their heart and soul.

   b. What did Moses remind the people that they had declared (v. 17)?

That the Lord was their God and that they would obey him.

   c. What did Moses say God had declared (vv. 18–19)?

That they were God's holy people, his treasured possession, and that he would set them high above all other nations.

Did You Know?

Success, not failure, is the greatest danger facing any follower of God, as Moses knew well. . . . Every significant downfall in his own life came when he seized power for himself—killing an Egyptian, smashing a rock in the desert—rather than relying on God.

—Philip Yancey

NOTES

Small Group Exploration: A Peculiar People

During the video presentation, Philip spoke about God calling the Hebrews "my peculiar people." They were to be different from any other nation. They were to think differently. They were to act differently. They were, in a nutshell, to be God's *holy* people, God's "set apart" people who would show others what God is like. Let's break into groups of three to five and take a look at a few passages in Deuteronomy that will help us understand what God had in mind for the people who would represent him to the world.

1. What was unique about the Hebrews? (See Deuteronomy 7:6–9.)

2. In Deuteronomy 7:12–14, we see how serious God considers his covenant to be. What did the Hebrews have to do in order to receive the benefits of God's covenant with them?

3. After Moses reviewed all the terms of God's covenant to the people, note what Moses emphasized. (See Deuteronomy 26:16–19.)
   a. What were the people to do (v. 16)?

   b. What did Moses remind the people that they had declared (v. 17)?

   c. What did Moses say God had declared (vv. 18–19)?

Did You Know?

Success, not failure, is the greatest danger facing any follower of God, as Moses knew well. . . . Every significant downfall in his own life came when he seized power for himself—killing an Egyptian, smashing a rock in the desert—rather than relying on God.

—Philip Yancey

4. We've seen how Moses emphasized the importance of the Hebrews knowing God's laws, applying those laws in daily life, and teaching those laws to their children. As Christians today, we, too, are to represent God to the world around us. To what extent do you think God's laws impact (or ought to impact) the way we live? How might our relationships with God and with other people change if we truly made obedience to God our overarching priority in daily life?

4. We've seen how Moses emphasized the importance of the Hebrews knowing God's laws, applying those laws in daily life, and teaching those laws to their children. As Christians today, we, too, are to represent God to the world around us. To what extent do you think God's laws impact (or ought to impact) the way we live? How might our relationships with God and with other people change if we truly made obedience to God our overarching priority in daily life?

There is no right or wrong answer here, but based on the video and the small group study these questions ought to promote meaningful discussion.

If you have divided into small groups, let participants know when there is 1 minute remaining.

Give participants a moment to transition from their small group discussions. If time allows, or if you have assigned each group a specific question, have representatives from the groups share their key ideas.

Now let's wrap up our Group Discovery time. Please turn to page 67.

Group Discussion (5 minutes)

Participant's Guide page 67.

Use one or more of the following questions to encourage participants to share their observations with the entire group.

1. Deuteronomy is essentially a record of the Hebrew people's oral history. In what ways does an oral history differ from what we might read in a textbook?

2. As modern people, we learn about history from textbooks. In what ways do we also create highlights or reviews of our history that function a bit like an oral history?

Examples might include the Jefferson Memorial, Civil War reenactments, the Holocaust Museum, etc.

What do these memorials of and monuments to our history do for us? In what ways do they change or influence our behavior?

Perspective

With the speeches in Deuteronomy, Moses established the great tradition of historical memory, a tradition his people, who became known as the Jews, have cherished ever since: "Never forget." Try as we might, we can never undo the past, but still we must honor it by bearing witness, by remembering so as not to allow it to repeat.

—Philip Yancey

3. What would you say is the most important thing for us to remember from this session?

NOTES

b. What did Moses remind the people that they had declared (v. 17)?

c. What did Moses say God had declared (vv. 18–19)?

Did You Know?

Success, not failure, is the greatest danger facing any follower of God, as Moses knew well. . . . Every significant downfall in his own life came when he seized power for himself—killing an Egyptian, smashing a rock in the desert—rather than relying on God.

—Philip Yancey

4. We've seen how Moses emphasized the importance of the Hebrews knowing God's laws, applying those laws in daily life, and teaching those laws to their children. As Christians today, we, too, are to represent God to the world around us. To what extent do you think God's laws impact (or ought to impact) the way we live? How might our relationships with God and with other people change if we truly made obedience to God our overarching priority in daily life?

Group Discussion

1. Deuteronomy is essentially a record of the Hebrew people's oral history. In what ways does an oral history differ from what we might read in a textbook?

2a. As modern people, we learn about history from textbooks. In what ways do we also create highlights or reviews of our history that function a bit like an oral history?

b. What do these memorials of and monuments to our history do for us? In what ways do they change or influence our behavior?

Perspective

With the speeches in Deuteronomy, Moses established the great tradition of historical memory, a tradition his people, who became known as the Jews, have cherished ever since: "Never forget." Try as we might, we can never undo the past, but still we must honor it by bearing witness, by remembering so as not to allow it to repeat.

—Philip Yancey

3. What would you say is the most important thing for us to remember from this session?

Independence Day

The United States celebrates July 4 like no other day. The parades, the picnics, and the fireworks boisterously express national pride. We showed 'em, say the politicians in their speeches. With our own sweat and blood we created a nation. We're proud to be Americans.

Our style of celebration—noisy and flag-waving and proud—captures something of the original spirit that led a young nation to declare independence. A similar spirit surges up in France on Bastille Day and in many other nations on their birthdays. But these celebrations bear a striking *unlikeness* to the Jewish independence day, a day called Passover.

The Jews trace their cultural birthday back to a dark, foreboding night—the Israelites' last in Egypt (Exodus 12). There are no blaring bands nor balloons nor fireworks to commemorate this event. Everything takes place inside a home, with a family or cluster of families gathered around a table. Participants taste morsels of food, pausing before each portion to hear Old Testament accounts of the history they are reliving. Their independence day resembles a worship service, not a party.

More than anything else, the Jewish independence day expresses this one fact: God did it. No Israelite armies stood against the mighty Egyptians. Freedom came in the blackest night while Israelite families huddled around the Passover table, their bags packed, waiting for deliverance.

—*The Student Bible*, 95

Independence Day

The United States celebrates July 4 like no other day. The parades, the picnics, and the fireworks boisterously express national pride. We showed 'em, say the politicians in their speeches. With our own sweat and blood we created a nation. We're proud to be Americans.

Our style of celebration—noisy and flag-waving and proud—captures something of the original spirit that led a young nation to declare independence. A similar spirit surges up in France on Bastille Day and in many other nations on their birthdays. But these celebrations bear a striking *unlikeness* to the Jewish independence day, a day called Passover.

The Jews trace their cultural birthday back to a dark, foreboding night—the Israelites' last in Egypt (Exodus 12). There are no blaring bands nor balloons nor fireworks to commemorate this event. Everything takes place inside a home, with a family or cluster of families gathered around a table. Participants taste morsels of food, pausing before each portion to hear Old Testament accounts of the history they are reliving. Their independence day resembles a worship service, not a party.

More than anything else, the Jewish independence day expresses this one fact: God did it. No Israelite armies stood against the mighty Egyptians. Freedom came in the blackest night while Israelite families huddled around the Passover table, their bags packed, waiting for deliverance.

—*The Student Bible,* 95

Now it's time for each of us to consider on a personal level what we've been discussing and thinking about. Please turn to page 69.

5 min. PERSONAL JOURNEY: TO BEGIN NOW

Participant's Guide page 69.

Deuteronomy records Moses' parting words as the Hebrews stood ready to cross the Jordan River and possess the Promised Land. Success–the land of milk and honey–was at last within their grasp, and Moses saw trouble ahead. He had learned that success is dangerous, so in the strongest terms he warned them to be careful.

Take some time now by yourself to reflect quietly on your walk with God and consider what God would have you do to remember what he has done for you in the past.

NOTES

3. What would you say is the most important thing for us to remember from this session?

Independence Day

The United States celebrates July 4 like no other day. The parades, the picnics, and the fireworks boisterously express national pride. We showed 'em, say the politicians in their speeches. With our own sweat and blood we created a nation. We're proud to be Americans.

Our style of celebration—noisy and flag-waving and proud—captures something of the original spirit that led a young nation to declare independence. A similar spirit surges up in France on Bastille Day and in many other nations on their birthdays. But these celebrations bear a striking *unlikeness* to the Jewish independence day, a day called Passover.

The Jews trace their cultural birthday back to a dark, foreboding night—the Israelites' last in Egypt (Exodus 12). There are no blaring bands nor balloons nor fireworks to commemorate this event. Everything takes place inside a home, with a family or cluster of families gathered around a table. Participants taste morsels of food, pausing before each portion to hear Old Testament accounts of the history they are reliving. Their independence day resembles a worship service, not a party.

More than anything else, the Jewish independence day expresses this one fact: God did it. No Israelite armies stood against the mighty Egyptians. Freedom came in the blackest night while Israelite families huddled around the Passover table, their bags packed, waiting for deliverance.

—*The Student Bible*, 95

Personal Journey: To Begin Now

Deuteronomy records Moses' parting words as the Hebrews stood ready to cross the Jordan River and possess the Promised Land. Success–the land of milk and honey–was at last within their grasp, and Moses saw trouble ahead. He had learned that success is dangerous, so in the strongest terms he warned them to be careful.

Take some time now by yourself to reflect quietly on your walk with God and consider what God would have you do to remember what he has done for you in the past.

1. When we are in trouble, we may find it easy to turn to God–for help, guidance, strength, and hope. But we often pay less attention to God, or ignore him altogether, when things are going well for us.

   a. What typically happens in your relationship with God when life is difficult?

   b. When life becomes more comfortable?

2a. If Moses knew you as well as he knew the Hebrews, what might be his concerns regarding your commitment to walk with God?

b. What might Moses' parting words be to you?

1. When we are in trouble, we may find it easy to turn to God—for help, guidance, strength, and hope. But we often pay less attention to God, or ignore him altogether, when things are going well for us.

   a. What typically happens in your relationship with God when life is difficult?

   b. When life becomes more comfortable?

2a. If Moses knew you as well as he knew the Hebrews, what might be his concerns regarding your commitment to walk with God?

   b. What might Moses' parting words be to you?

Let participants know when there is 1 minute remaining. Remind participants that they may want to continue their journey by completing the additional exercise on page 70 of their Participant's Guide before the next session.

PERSONAL JOURNEY: TO DO BETWEEN SESSIONS

Over and over again, Moses commanded the people not to forget about God. The tired old man who talked with God challenged them to remember what God had done for them. He reminded them that God had chosen them to be his holy people. He urged them to remember where they had been so they could go where they were destined to go.

Before the next session, set aside time away from distractions to do the following exercise.

1. God wants a personal relationship with us. He wants us not to forget what he has done for us in the past, what he is doing for us today, and what he will do for us tomorrow. What comes between you and God that keeps you from remembering and acting on the presence of God in your life?

Perspective

Life with God is never so easy, so settled, for any of us. Not for the Hebrews then, and not for us living today. The pilgrim must ever progress, uphill, meeting new enemies around every bend.

—Philip Yancey

NOTES

Personal Journey: To Begin Now

Deuteronomy records Moses' parting words as the Hebrews stood ready to cross the Jordan River and possess the Promised Land. Success—the land of milk and honey—was at last within their grasp, and Moses saw trouble ahead. He had learned that success is dangerous, so in the strongest terms he warned them to be careful.

Take some time now by yourself to reflect quietly on your walk with God and consider what God would have you do to remember what he has done for you in the past.

1. When we are in trouble, we may find it easy to turn to God—for help, guidance, strength, and hope. But we often pay less attention to God, or ignore him altogether, when things are going well for us.
   a. What typically happens in your relationship with God when life is difficult?
   b. When life becomes more comfortable?

2a. If Moses knew you as well as he knew the Hebrews, what might be his concerns regarding your commitment to walk with God?

b. What might Moses' parting words be to you?

Personal Journey: To Do between Sessions

Over and over again, Moses commanded the people not to forget about God. The tired old man who talked with God challenged them to remember what God had done for them. He reminded them that God had chosen them to be his holy people. He urged them to remember where they had been so they could go where they were destined to go.

1. God wants a personal relationship with us. He wants us not to forget what he has done for us in the past, what he is doing for us today, and what he will do for us tomorrow. What comes between you and God that keeps you from remembering and acting on the presence of God in your life?

Perspective

Life with God is never so easy, so settled, for any of us. Not for the Hebrews then, and not for us living today. The pilgrim must ever progress, uphill, meeting new enemies around every bend.

—Philip Yancey

2. Moses and the elders established a variety of activities to help keep God and his laws foremost in the minds of his people (Deuteronomy 16, 27). Which activities would help focus your heart and mind toward God and on what it means to obey him? Which of those activities, or spiritual disciplines, do you presently practice? Which of those activities might you want to add to your life?

3. If you were to erect "standing stones" to commemorate God's faithfulness to you, how many different piles would you have to build? What would each of them commemorate?

God's Personal Nature

During his experience with God and the Israelites, Moses rediscovered a fundamental fact about God: He is a person. Whereas the Egyptians and Canaanites viewed their gods as distant, unapproachable, capricious, and unpredictable, the Israelites grew to understand that their God was quite different. Their God:

- Was as personal as they themselves
- Spoke to them and listened to them
- Felt pain and jealousy when his people were unfaithful
- Negotiated and signed contracts
- Expressed his love for humanity
- Insisted on holiness but was also willing to forgive
- Established boundaries for behavior that could be understood and obeyed
- Gave out mercy as well as discipline
- Desired honor
- Longed for his covenant with the Hebrews to succeed
- Met with Moses face to face

1 min. CLOSING MEDITATION

Let's take a moment to close in prayer.

Dear God, thank you for being a personal God who loves us and wants to be in relationship with us. Please help us walk according to your truths, to seek you with all our hearts. Fill our hearts with praise to you for all that you have done, all that you are doing, and all that you will do in our lives. Teach us what it means to hide your Word in our hearts so that we won't sin against you. Help us to receive the true joy that comes from obeying you and trusting in you. In Jesus' name we pray, amen.

—Prayer inspired by Psalm 119:1–16

NOTES

2. Moses and the elders established a variety of activities to help keep God and his laws foremost in the minds of his people (Deuteronomy 16, 27). Which activities would help focus your heart and mind toward God and on what it means to obey him? Which of those activities, or spiritual disciplines, do you presently practice? Which of those activities might you want to add to your life?

3. If you were to erect "standing stones" to commemorate God's faithfulness to you, how many different piles would you have to build? What would each of them commemorate?

God's Personal Nature

During his experience with God and the Israelites, Moses rediscovered a fundamental fact about God: He is a person. Whereas the Egyptians and Canaanites viewed their gods as distant, unapproachable, capricious, and unpredictable, the Israelites grew to understand that their God was quite different. Their God:

- Was as personal as they themselves
- Spoke to them and listened to them
- Felt pain and jealousy when his people were unfaithful
- Negotiated and signed contracts
- Expressed his love for humanity
- Insisted on holiness but was also willing to forgive
- Established boundaries for behavior that could be understood and obeyed
- Gave out mercy as well as discipline
- Desired honor
- Longed for his covenant with the Hebrews to succeed
- Met with Moses face to face

SESSION FIVE

Psalms: Spirituality in Every Key

BEFORE YOU LEAD

Synopsis

Written during what could be considered Israel's "golden age," the book of Psalms is a remarkable anthology of literature that expresses the ups and downs of spiritual life. Like all great literature, the book of Psalms transcends time and culture. Some people consider it to be their favorite book of the Bible while others find it confusing, repetitive, or even depressing. Regardless of personal opinion, however, the psalms have stood the test of time for more than three thousand years. It is truly amazing to realize that when we recite and sing the psalms today, we are reciting and singing the same poems that were written during David and Solomon's era!

But the message of the book of Psalms can be hard for contemporary Christians to grasp. The 150 psalms in the book of Psalms seem to contradict each other in a wild, roller-coaster ride through despair, joy, and praise. This is because they are actually a compilation of prayers to God written by different people over a period of time. There is no overarching principle, point, or theme that we are supposed to learn from reading the psalms; rather, as Kathleen Norris observes in her book *The Cloister Walk*, "The psalms are poetry, and poetry's function is not to explain but to offer images and stories that resonate with our lives."

We need the images of the psalms to help us honestly express to God our feelings and our understanding of the world in which we live. "When I look at the psalms especially," Philip Yancey says, "I get the impression that God understands it's hard for us to get the hard stuff out." He goes on to say, "So many times it's hard for me to come up with my own words to express my feelings, and the psalms become a guidebook for me. I don't have to come up with my own words. They are already there.... I turn those very words into my own personal prayer to God."

Perhaps, as you will discover through this session, the greatest contribution of the psalms is that they cover the entire spectrum of our relationship with God and help us express ourselves to him. And it's up to us, as readers, to find the individual psalms that speak to us wherever we are in our journey with God.

Key Points of This Session

1. The book of Psalms comprises a remarkable anthology of literature that has had an impact on the Jewish and Christian faiths for more than 3,000 years! The psalms do not exist primarily to tell a story or teach principles of doctrine; they are, instead, a collection of personal letters to God that show us what relationship with God looks like. In a deeply personal way, the psalms help us reconcile what we believe about life with what we actually encounter in life.

2. The 150 psalms cover the entire spectrum of our relationship with God—the happy times, times of praise, the sad times, times of woundedness, and times of confusion. As such, these prayers in poetry can help us honestly express our feelings to God, including feelings we may find difficult to express, such as rage, doubt, paranoia, meanness, delight, joy, praise, and betrayal.

Suggested Reading

This session corresponds to Chapter 4 of *The Bible Jesus Read.* You may want to read this chapter in order to deepen your understanding of this material.

Session Outline (52 minutes)

I. Introduction (5 minutes)
   A. Welcome
   B. What's to Come
   C. Questions to Think About
II. Video Presentation: "Psalms: Spirituality in Every Key" (11 minutes)
III. Group Discovery (30 minutes)
   A. Video Highlights (5 minutes)
   B. Large Group Exploration: Understanding an Anthology of Personal Letters (10 minutes)
   C. Small Group Exploration: A Guidebook for Sharing Our Hearts with God (10 minutes)
   D. Group Discussion (5 minutes)
IV. Personal Journey (5 minutes)
V. Closing Meditation (1 minute)

Materials

You'll need a VCR, TV, and Bible. You may also find a whiteboard, flip chart, or overhead projector to be a useful tool in guiding group discussion. View the video prior to leading the session so you are familiar with its main points.

SESSION FIVE

Psalms: Spirituality in Every Key

> Poetry works its magic subtly. . . . We turn to it because the poet's shaping of words and images gives us pleasure and moves our emotions. Yet if the poet succeeds, we may gain something greater than knowledge: a transformed vision. That is the magic the psalms have ultimately worked upon me. They have transformed my spiritual vision and my understanding of relationship with God.
>
> —Philip Yancey

5 min. INTRODUCTION

Welcome

Welcome participants to Session 5 of *The Bible Jesus Read* course: "Psalms: Spirituality in Every Key."

What's to Come

During this session, we'll be introduced to the book of Psalms, a remarkable anthology of literature that has had an impact on the Jewish and Christian faiths for more than 3,000 years! The 150 psalms do not exist primarily to tell a story or teach principles of doctrine; they are, instead, a collection of personal letters to God that show us what relationship with God looks like. As such, these prayers in poetry cover the entire spectrum of our relationship with God and can help us honestly express our deepest feelings to him.

Let's begin by considering a few questions. Please turn to page 73 of your Participant's Guide.

Questions to Think About

Participant's Guide page 73.

As time permits, ask two or more of the following questions and solicit responses from the participants.

NOTES

SESSION FIVE

Psalms: Spirituality in Every Key

> Poetry works its magic subtly. . . . We turn to it because the poet's shaping of words and images gives us pleasure and moves our emotions. Yet if the poet succeeds, we may gain something greater than knowledge: a transformed vision. That is the magic the psalms have ultimately worked upon me. They have transformed my spiritual vision and my understanding of relationship with God.
>
> —Philip Yancey

Questions to Think About

1. What has been your experience in reading the psalms, and what do you expect to find when you read them?

2. How do your perceptions of and feelings toward the psalms change when you read just a few of them in contrast to when you try to read a number of them straight through?

3. Would you dare to say to God some of the things the psalmists have said? Why or why not?

73

1. What has been your experience in reading the psalms, and what do you expect to find when you read them?

The intent here is to encourage participants to share a variety of experiences and expectations concerning the psalms. Some participants may tell of receiving great blessing from their reading, some may have been encouraged, and others may have been confused or even discouraged. Participants' previous experiences with the psalms will tend to predispose them toward certain expectations.

2. How do your perceptions of and feelings toward the psalms change when you read just a few of them in contrast to when you try to read a number of them straight through?

Again, encourage participants to share their experiences. Because of the varied and extreme emotions freely expressed from psalm to psalm, many people become confused when they read a great number of psalms within a short time span. Because the book of Psalms is an anthology, there is no consistent theme or argument, so the psalms may seem disjointed and unrelated. When a theme is repeated in psalm after psalm, the repetition can seem oppressive. It is not uncommon for people who enjoy the psalms in small doses to become confused, frustrated, or even angry when trying to read many of them in a short time span.

3. Would you dare to say to God some of the things the psalmists have said? Why or why not?

Note: Be aware that some participants may not have read many of the psalms.

Explore with participants how honest we are willing to be with God. Discuss whether or not God will really "take" what we may want to "dish out."

Let's keep these ideas in mind as we view the video. There is space to take notes on page 74.

11 min. VIDEO PRESENTATION: "PSALMS: SPIRITUALITY IN EVERY KEY"

Participant's Guide page 74.

Leader's Video Observations

The psalms:

Prayers about life with God

NOTES

SESSION FIVE

Psalms: Spirituality in Every Key

> Poetry works its magic subtly. . . . We turn to it because the poet's shaping of words and images gives us pleasure and moves our emotions. Yet if the poet succeeds, we may gain something greater than knowledge: a transformed vision. That is the magic the psalms have ultimately worked upon me. They have transformed my spiritual vision and my understanding of relationship with God.
>
> —Philip Yancey

Questions to Think About

1. What has been your experience in reading the psalms, and what do you expect to find when you read them?

2. How do your perceptions of and feelings toward the psalms change when you read just a few of them in contrast to when you try to read a number of them straight through?

3. Would you dare to say to God some of the things the psalmists have said? Why or why not?

Video Presentation: "The Psalms: Spirituality in Every Key"

The psalms:

- Prayers about life with God

- Timeless poetry from a "golden age"

- Deeply honest expression before God

Reading the psalms

Timeless poetry from a "golden age"

Deeply honest expression before God

Reading the psalms

30 min. GROUP DISCOVERY

If your group has seven or more members, use the Video Highlights with the entire group (5 minutes), then complete the Large Group Exploration (10 minutes), and then break into small groups of three to five people for the Small Group Exploration (10 minutes). Finally, bring everyone together for the closing Group Discussion (5 minutes).

If your group has fewer than seven members, begin with the Video Highlights (5 minutes), then complete both the Large Group Exploration (10 minutes) and the Small Group Exploration (10 minutes) as a group. Wrap up your discovery time with the Group Discussion (5 minutes).

Please turn to page 75 as we discuss some questions related to the video segment we have just seen.

Video Highlights (5 minutes)

Participant's Guide page 75.

As time permits, ask one or more of the following questions, which directly relate to the video the participants have just seen.

Note: If your time is limited, you may want to do Question 3 first.

1. Philip Yancey said he sometimes finds it hard to express his deepest feelings to God and that the book of Psalms has become a guidebook for him, helping him to express in words what he is feeling. What do you think about this idea? Why?

NOTES

Video Presentation: "The Psalms: Spirituality in Every Key"

The psalms:
Prayers about life with God

Timeless poetry from a "golden age"

Deeply honest expression before God

Reading the psalms

Video Highlights

1. Philip Yancey said he sometimes finds it hard to express his deepest feelings to God and that the book of Psalms has become a guidebook for him, helping him to express in words what he is feeling. What do you think about this idea? Why?

2. What do you think would be the benefit of Philip Yancey's suggestion that we search the psalms until we find one that reflects where we are at a given moment—and then meditate on that particular psalm?

3. The following chart gives a few references to the psalms from the book of Matthew. How does it affect your appreciation of the psalms to realize that God's people have read, memorized, sung, discussed, and pondered these expressive prayers to God for thousands of years?

This question introduces an important concept. Some participants may not have read more than a few psalms, while others may have memorized and prayed a number of psalms. Those who are more familiar with the psalms may find it easier to understand the "guidebook" viewpoint. One way the psalms help us express our feelings to God is by showing us that someone has "gone on before us" and has expressed feelings similar to our own. Because of this, we feel invited to share our deepest feelings with God as well.

2. What do you think would be the benefit of Philip Yancey's suggestion that we search the psalms until we find one that reflects where we are at a given moment–and then meditate on that particular psalm?

Because the psalms reflect so many emotional ups and downs (from praise to utter despair), different psalms will speak to us at different times. It is important to share our deepest feelings—the good and the bad, the safe and the risky—with God. The expressiveness of the psalms can help us identify, understand, and share those feelings.

3. The following chart gives a few references to the psalms from the book of Matthew. How does it affect your appreciation of the psalms to realize that God's people have read, memorized, sung, discussed, and pondered these expressive prayers to God for thousands of years? What is your response when you realize that the words of a psalm that expresses what you are thinking or feeling today were penned about 3,000 years ago?

Most participants have never thought about the psalms in this way. The impact of the psalms through 3,000 years of history is truly mind-boggling. Some participants will be especially impressed by the freshness of raw emotional expression that was actually written thousands of years ago. They may wonder how someone who lived thousands of years ago could know exactly how they feel!

Did You Know?

The New Testament books include many references to the book of Psalms. Some of these references occur in conversations Jesus had with other people, while other references were chosen by various New Testament authors to make a point. It is obvious from these New Testament references that phrases and ideas from the psalms were well known and commonly used by the general public of Jesus' day. The following list highlights just a few such references found in the book of Matthew.

New Testament Link to a Psalm	Psalm Source
Matthew 4:6—Satan quoted from Psalm 91 when he tempted Jesus	Psalm 91:11–12
Matthew 13:35—Matthew recognized that Jesus' words were a fulfillment of the prophecy: "I will open my mouth in parables, I will utter things hidden . . . ."	Psalm 78:2

NOTES

Video Highlights

1. Philip Yancey said he sometimes finds it hard to express his deepest feelings to God and that the book of Psalms has become a guidebook for him, helping him to express in words what he is feeling. What do you think about this idea? Why?

2. What do you think would be the benefit of Philip Yancey's suggestion that we search the psalms until we find one that reflects where we are at a given moment–and then meditate on that particular psalm?

3. The following chart gives a few references to the psalms from the book of Matthew. How does it affect your appreciation of the psalms to realize that God's people have read, memorized, sung, discussed, and pondered these expressive prayers to God for thousands of years?

What is your response when you realize that the words of a psalm that expresses what you are thinking or feeling today were penned about 3,000 years ago?

Did You Know?

The New Testament books include many references to the book of Psalms. Some of these references occur in conversations Jesus had with other people, while other references were chosen by various New Testament authors to make a point. It is obvious from these New Testament references that phrases and ideas from the psalms were well known and commonly used by the general public of Jesus' day. The following list highlights just a few such references found in the book of Matthew.

New Testament Link to a Psalm	Psalm Source
Matthew 4:6—Satan quoted from Psalm 91 when he tempted Jesus	Psalm 91:11–12
Matthew 13:35—Matthew recognized that Jesus' words were a fulfillment of the prophecy: "I will open my mouth in parables, I will utter things hidden . . . ."	Psalm 78:2
Matthew 21:42—Jesus quoted from Psalm 118 when asking a key question	Psalm 118:22–23
Matthew 22:44—Jesus used the first verse of Psalm 110 to confound some Pharisees	Psalm 110:1
Matthew 23:39—Jesus reveals his extensive knowledge of the psalms	Psalm 118:26
Matthew 27:46—Matthew recorded Jesus' words, realizing that they fulfilled a prophecy from Psalm 22	Psalm 22:1

New Testament Link to a Psalm	Psalm Source
Matthew 21:42—Jesus quoted from Psalm 118 when asking a key question	Psalm 118:22–23
Matthew 22:44—Jesus used the first verse of Psalm 110 to confound some Pharisees	Psalm 110:1
Matthew 23:39—Jesus reveals his extensive knowledge of the psalms	Psalm 118:26
Matthew 27:46—Matthew recorded Jesus' words, realizing that they fulfilled a prophecy from Psalm 22	Psalm 22:1

Now we're ready for the Large Group Exploration part of this session. Please turn to page 77.

Large Group Exploration: Understanding an Anthology of Personal Letters (10 minutes)

Participant's Guide page 77.

Read the introductory paragraph to the group, then begin discussing the questions that follow.

Philip Yancey writes, "For the Hebrew poets, God represented a reality more solid than their own whipsaw emotions or the checkered history of their people. They wrestled with God over every facet of their lives, and in the end it was the very act of wrestling that proved their faith." One way to approach the book of Psalms is to think of it as a collection of personal letters that, when put together, reveals a panoramic picture of humanity wrestling with God. Let's consider the perspective these letters provide.

1. In what ways does approaching the book of Psalms as an anthology of poetry change your expectations for this book?

This certainly relieves a heavy burden that evangelical Christianity often places on the psalms. With the anthology viewpoint, we no longer expect the psalms to provide "answers" or a specific doctrinal lesson. Nor do we expect the book to fit a progressive outline of theological instruction. Instead, the anthology viewpoint allows individual psalms to speak to us about life within the context of our personal relationship with God.

2. Part of what the psalms give us is a unique look into David's soul—the soul of a man who loved God. Various psalms reveal his delight, his frustration, and the ways in which he reconciled the events of his life with what he knew of God. Let's take a quick look at some circumstances of David's life and the psalms he wrote during those times.

Note: The circumstances are summarized below for your convenience. If time permits, you may want to read both the circumstances as well as David's responses to those circumstances in the psalms.

NOTES

What is your response when you realize that the words of a psalm that expresses what you are thinking or feeling today were penned about 3,000 years ago?

Did You Know?

The New Testament books include many references to the book of Psalms. Some of these references occur in conversations Jesus had with other people, while other references were chosen by various New Testament authors to make a point. It is obvious from these New Testament references that phrases and ideas from the psalms were well known and commonly used by the general public of Jesus' day. The following list highlights just a few such references found in the book of Matthew.

New Testament Link to a Psalm	Psalm Source
Matthew 4:6—Satan quoted from Psalm 91 when he tempted Jesus	Psalm 91:11–12
Matthew 13:35—Matthew recognized that Jesus' words were a fulfillment of the prophecy: "I will open my mouth in parables, I will utter things hidden . . . ."	Psalm 78:2
Matthew 21:42—Jesus quoted from Psalm 118 when asking a key question	Psalm 118:22–23
Matthew 22:44—Jesus used the first verse of Psalm 110 to confound some Pharisees	Psalm 110:1
Matthew 23:39—Jesus reveals his extensive knowledge of the psalms	Psalm 118:26
Matthew 27:46—Matthew recorded Jesus' words, realizing that they fulfilled a prophecy from Psalm 22	Psalm 22:1

Large Group Exploration: Understanding an Anthology of Personal Letters

Philip Yancey writes, "For the Hebrew poets, God represented a reality more solid than their own whipsaw emotions or the checkered history of their people. They wrestled with God over every facet of their lives, and in the end it was the very act of wrestling that proved their faith." One way to approach the book of Psalms is to think of it as a collection of personal letters that, when put together, reveals a panoramic picture of humanity wrestling with God. Let's consider the perspective these letters provide.

1. In what ways does approaching the book of Psalms as an anthology of poetry change your expectations for this book?

2. Part of what the psalms give us is a unique look into David's soul—the soul of a man who loved God. Various psalms reveal his delight, his frustration, and the ways in which he reconciled the events of his life with what he knew of God. Let's take a quick look at some circumstances of David's life and the psalms he wrote during those times.

Circumstances of David's Life: His Outward Journey	**The Psalms David Wrote: His Inward Journey**
1 Samuel 21:10–15: David feigns madness in a successful attempt to keep from being killed by the Philistines.	Psalm 56: David is in great danger, but he credits God for delivering his soul from death and keeping his feet from stumbling.
1 Samuel 19:1–17: David sneaks out of a window while his wife diverts pursuers sent by King Saul to kill him.	Psalm 59: David's life is threatened, but he gives God the credit for being his fortress and his loving God.
1 and 2 Samuel: David is chased around by his enemies for years and has to fight all-night battles.	Psalm 18: David, despite life-threatening situations, seems confident of God's miraculous deliverance.
2 Samuel 12:1–14: Nathan confronted David concerning his sin with Bathsheba and his murder of her husband, Uriah.	Psalm 51: David recognizes his sin as an offense to God and asks for God's mercy and cleansing, but he also recognizes his sinful human state and God's desire for relationship.

a. As you compare each psalm to the circumstance in which David wrote it, what relationship do you see between the psalm and the situation in which it was written? Do you find what you expected?

Participants may be surprised by what they see. The psalms don't necessarily match up in the way we might expect. We might think, for example, from reading a particular psalm that God did a miracle on David's behalf, yet David's deliverance may appear to us to be more a result of David's ingenuity than divine intervention. The important concept here is that David instinctively relates the situations of his life to God.

b. What do you discover from these psalms about David's view of God's work in his life?

David focused on a bigger picture than his immediate circumstances. In David's view, God was clearly on center stage. David recognized that God was intimately involved in the details of his life—David was a player in the orchestra, but God was the composer and conductor.

c. What did David express that reveals his confidence that he mattered to God? (See Psalm 18:19.)

David wrote, "He [God] rescued me because he delighted in me."

NOTES

Circumstances of David's Life: His Outward Journey	The Psalms David Wrote: His Inward Journey
1 Samuel 21:10–15: David feigns madness in a successful attempt to keep from being killed by the Philistines.	Psalm 56:
1 Samuel 19:1–17: David sneaks out of a window while his wife diverts pursuers sent by King Saul to kill him.	Psalm 59:
1 and 2 Samuel: David is chased around by his enemies for years and has to fight all-night battles.	Psalm 18:
2 Samuel 12:1–14: Nathan confronted David concerning his sin with Bathsheba and his murder of her husband, Uriah.	Psalm 51:

a. As you compare each psalm to the circumstance in which David wrote it, what relationship do you see between the psalm and the situation in which it was written? Do you find what you expected?

b. What do you discover from these psalms about David's view of God's work in his life?

c. What did David express that reveals his confidence that he mattered to God? (See Psalm 18:19.)

Perspective

In my fixation with the details of the psalms . . . I had missed the main point, which is that the book of Psalms comprises a sampling of spiritual journals, much like personal letters to God. . . . They are personal prayers in the form of poetry, written by a variety of people—peasants, kings, professional musicians, rank amateurs—in wildly fluctuating moods. . . . examples of "ordinary" people struggling mightily to align what they believe about God with what they actually experience.

—Philip Yancey

Perspective

In my fixation with the details of the psalms ... I had missed the main point, which is that the book of Psalms comprises a sampling of spiritual journals, much like personal letters to God.... They are personal prayers in the form of poetry, written by a variety of people—peasants, kings, professional musicians, rank amateurs—in wildly fluctuating moods.... examples of "ordinary" people struggling mightily to align what they believe about God with what they actually experience.

—Philip Yancey

Please turn to page 80 as we move into the Small Group Exploration part of this session.

Small Group Exploration: A Guidebook for Sharing Our Hearts with God (10 minutes)

Participant's Guide page 80.

God wants us to express our deepest feelings to him, not to pretend to be something we are not. "Doubt, paranoia, giddiness, meanness, delight, hatred, joy, praise, vengefulness, betrayal–you can find it all in Psalms," Philip Yancey writes. "Such strewing of emotions, which I once saw as hopeless disarray, I now see as a sign of health. From Psalms I have learned that I can rightfully bring to God whatever I feel about him. I need not paper over my failures and try to clean up my own rottenness; far better to bring those weaknesses to God, who alone has the power to heal."

Let's break into groups of three to five and look more closely at the emotions expressed in a few psalms.

If you will not be breaking into small groups for the Small Group Exploration, lead the group in a discussion of the following questions.

1. Poetry is an expression of the soul–the thoughts and feelings that resonate deep within our hearts. Let's look at a sampling of passages from the book of Psalms and note the range and depth of emotion the psalmists express to God.

   a. Psalm 13:1–4

Feeling as if God has forgotten and doesn't care about the psalmist's troubles.

   b. Psalm 30:11–12

Feelings of great joy and thankfulness for what God had done in the psalmist's life.

NOTES

b. What do you discover from these psalms about David's view of God's work in his life?

c. What did David express that reveals his confidence that he mattered to God? (See Psalm 18:19.)

Perspective

In my fixation with the details of the psalms . . . I had missed the main point, which is that the book of Psalms comprises a sampling of spiritual journals, much like personal letters to God. . . . They are personal prayers in the form of poetry, written by a variety of people—peasants, kings, professional musicians, rank amateurs—in wildly fluctuating moods. . . . examples of "ordinary" people struggling mightily to align what they believe about God with what they actually experience.

—Philip Yancey

Small Group Exploration: A Guidebook for Sharing Our Hearts with God

God wants us to express our deepest feelings to him, not to pretend to be something we are not. "Doubt, paranoia, giddiness, meanness, delight, hatred, joy, praise, vengefulness, betrayal—you can find it all in Psalms," Philip Yancey writes. "Such strewing of emotions, which I once saw as hopeless disarray, I now see as a sign of health. From Psalms I have learned that I can rightfully bring to God whatever I feel about him. I need not paper over my failures and try to clean up my own rottenness; far better to bring those weaknesses to God, who alone has the power to heal."

Let's break into groups of three to five and look more closely at the emotions expressed in a few psalms.

1. Poetry is an expression of the soul—the thoughts and feelings that resonate deep within our hearts. Let's look at a sampling of passages from the book of Psalms and note the range and depth of emotion the psalmists express to God.

   a. Psalm 13:1–4

   b. Psalm 30:11–12

   c. Psalm 34:4–22

c. Psalm 34:4–22

An intimate expression of personal relationship with God, a vivid recognition of and appreciation for the relationship between God and the righteous.

d. Psalm 38:1–15

Powerful feelings of guilt and anguish of heart presented before God, and a waiting for God to respond.

e. Psalm 42

Personal soul-searching, deep feelings of depression and even despair. Yet even in these depths, there is a backdrop of hope in relationship with God.

f. Psalm 58

A vivid, violent request for God to take vengeance on the wicked.

2. In what way(s) have you been encouraged to express or discouraged from expressing what you really think and feel to God? How might understanding the book of Psalms as a collection of heartfelt poems or letters written to God encourage you to share more honestly with God?

The intent here is to encourage participants to evaluate the integrity of their communication with God and to explore any hindrances to honest communication with him. Some participants may still hesitate to open their hearts, to be truly vulnerable to God. But some may begin to see how honestly others communicate and may be encouraged to do so themselves.

The church does not always give people the freedom to really share their heartaches and struggles. Consequently many Christians have two faces—the one they present to other people and the real one. Many Christians carry that into their relationship with God and seem to feel that God can't (or doesn't want to) handle their "ugly" feelings.

If you have divided into small groups, let participants know when there is 1 minute remaining.

Give participants a moment to transition from their small group discussions. If time allows, or if you have assigned each group a specific question, have representatives from the groups share their key ideas.

Now let's wrap up our Group Discovery time. Please turn to page 82.

Perspective

More than any other book in the Bible, Psalms reveals what a heartfelt, soul-starved, single-minded relationship with God looks like.

—Philip Yancey

NOTES

Small Group Exploration: A Guidebook for Sharing Our Hearts with God

God wants us to express our deepest feelings to him, not to pretend to be something we are not. "Doubt, paranoia, giddiness, meanness, delight, hatred, joy, praise, vengefulness, betrayal—you can find it all in Psalms," Philip Yancey writes. "Such strewing of emotions, which I once saw as hopeless disarray, I now see as a sign of health. From Psalms I have learned that I can rightfully bring to God whatever I feel about him. I need not paper over my failures and try to clean up my own rottenness; far better to bring those weaknesses to God, who alone has the power to heal."

Let's break into groups of three to five and look more closely at the emotions expressed in a few psalms.

1. Poetry is an expression of the soul—the thoughts and feelings that resonate deep within our hearts. Let's look at a sampling of passages from the book of Psalms and note the range and depth of emotion the psalmists express to God.

   a. Psalm 13:1–4

   b. Psalm 30:11–12

   c. Psalm 34:4–22

   d. Psalm 38:1–15

   e. Psalm 42

   f. Psalm 58

2. In what way(s) have you been encouraged to express or discouraged from expressing what you really think and feel to God? How might understanding the book of Psalms as a collection of heartfelt poems or letters written to God encourage you to share more honestly with God?

Perspective

More than any other book in the Bible, Psalms reveals what a heart-felt, soul-starved, single-minded relationship with God looks like.
—Philip Yancey

Group Discussion (5 minutes)

Participant's Guide page 82.

Use one or more of the following questions to encourage participants to share their observations with the entire group.

1. The book of Psalms comprises a remarkable anthology of literature that has had an impact on the Jewish and Christian faiths for more than 3,000 years! As we've seen, the psalms do not exist primarily to tell a story or teach principles of doctrine; they are, instead, a collection of personal letters to God that show us what relationship with God looks like. In a deeply personal way, they help us reconcile what we believe about life with what we actually encounter in life. Why is it important for us to reorient our daily experiences to the spiritual world—to the reality of God and our relationship with him?

2. The 150 psalms cover the entire spectrum of our relationship with God—times of happiness, times of praise, times of sadness, times of woundedness, and even times of confusion. As such, these prayers in poetry can help us honestly express our feelings to God, including feelings we may find difficult to express such as rage, doubt, paranoia, meanness, delight, joy, praise, and betrayal. In what ways might we benefit from using the psalms to bring our deepest feelings to God?

Now it's time for each of us to consider on a personal level what we've been discussing and thinking about. Please turn to page 83.

5 min. PERSONAL JOURNEY: TO BEGIN NOW

Participant's Guide page 83.

Even if it is little more than a vague memory of Psalm 23, nearly all of us have some exposure to the book of Psalms. Take some time now by yourself to quietly consider what else the psalms might offer you as you grow in your walk with God.

1. At one point in his efforts to understand the book of Psalms, Philip Yancey wrote, "People around me used the book as a spiritual medicine cabinet ... an approach that never worked for me. With uncanny consistency I would land on a psalm that aggravated, rather than cured, my problem. Martin Marty judges at least half the psalms to be 'wintry' in tone, and when feeling low I would accidentally turn to one of the wintriest and end up frostily depressed."

   a. How would you describe your personal experience with the psalms thus far?

NOTES

Group Discussion

1. The book of Psalms comprises a remarkable anthology of literature that has had an impact on the Jewish and Christian faiths for more than 3,000 years! As we've seen, the psalms do not exist primarily to tell a story or teach principles of doctrine; they are, instead, a collection of personal letters to God that show us what relationship with God looks like. In a deeply personal way, they help us reconcile what we believe about life with what we actually encounter in life. Why is it important for us to reorient our daily experiences to the spiritual world—to the reality of God and our relationship with him?

2. The 150 psalms cover the entire spectrum of our relationship with God—the happy times, times of praise, the sad times, times of woundedness, and times of confusion. As such, these prayers in poetry can help us honestly express our feelings to God, including feelings we may find difficult to express such as rage, doubt, paranoia, meanness, delight, joy, praise, and betrayal. In what ways might we benefit from using the psalms to bring our deepest feelings to God?

Personal Journey: To Begin Now

Even if it is little more than a vague memory of Psalm 23, nearly all of us have some exposure to the book of Psalms. Take some time now by yourself to quietly consider what else the psalms might offer you as you grow in your walk with God.

1. At one point in his efforts to understand the book of Psalms, Philip Yancey wrote, "People around me used the book as a spiritual medicine cabinet ... an approach that never worked for me. With uncanny consistency I would land on a psalm that aggravated, rather than cured, my problem. Martin Marty judges at least half the psalms to be 'wintry' in tone, and when feeling low I would accidentally turn to one of the wintriest and end up frostily depressed."

   a. How would you describe your personal experience with the psalms thus far?

   b. If your experience with the psalms has been less than satisfying to you, what have you learned during this session that may help you experience the psalms in a new way?

b. If your experience with the psalms has been less than satisfying to you, what have you learned during this session that may help you experience the psalms in a new way?

2. Much of this session has focused on the importance of expressing the depth of our thoughts and feelings about life to God.

   a. In what ways has this session encouraged you to be more honest and open in your relationship with God?

   b. What makes it difficult for you to really level with God about your deepest pain, struggles, and insecurities?

   c. What do you want to do about these obstacles?

Let participants know when there is 1 minute remaining. Remind participants that they may want to continue their journey by completing the additional exercise on page 85 of their Participant's Guide before the next session.

PERSONAL JOURNEY: TO DO BETWEEN SESSIONS

Many of us feel overwhelmed at the prospect of actually writing a psalm, but if we view it as a process of focusing on God and honestly expressing our thoughts, questions, and feelings about how our lives relate to him, it might not be so hard after all. The steps listed below will help guide you through the process of writing a psalm to God about your life and relationship with him.

Before the next session, set aside time away from distractions to do the following exercise.

1. *What significant things—events, people, places, thoughts—are happening in my life?* Look at a portion of your life. It could be what happened today, during the past week, or even a short segment of any time in your life. It could be a situation that inspired great joy or great sorrow. Write out several short phrases or one-word descriptions of what happened, your thoughts, your feelings, which objects or events were involved, your questions for God:

   Object or event:

   My feelings:

   What I think/thought:

   Questions for God:

NOTES

Personal Journey: To Begin Now

Even if it is little more than a vague memory of Psalm 23, nearly all of us have some exposure to the book of Psalms. Take some time now by yourself to quietly consider what else the psalms might offer you as you grow in your walk with God.

1. At one point in his efforts to understand the book of Psalms, Philip Yancey wrote, "People around me used the book as a spiritual medicine cabinet ... an approach that never worked for me. With uncanny consistency I would land on a psalm that aggravated, rather than cured, my problem. Martin Marty judges at least half the psalms to be 'wintry' in tone, and when feeling low I would accidentally turn to one of the wintriest and end up frostily depressed."
   a. How would you describe your personal experience with the psalms thus far?

   b. If your experience with the psalms has been less than satisfying to you, what have you learned during this session that may help you experience the psalms in a new way?

2. Much of this session has focused on the importance of expressing the depth of our thoughts and feelings about life to God.
   a. In what ways has this session encouraged you to be more honest and open in your relationship with God?

   b. What makes it difficult for you to really level with God about your deepest pain, struggles, and insecurities?

   c. What do you want to do about these obstacles?

Personal Journey: To Do between Sessions

Many of us feel overwhelmed at the prospect of actually writing a psalm, but if we view it as a process of focusing on God and honestly expressing our thoughts, questions, and feelings about how our lives relate to him, it might not be so hard after all. The steps listed below will help guide you through the process of writing a psalm to God about your life and relationship with him.

1. *What significant things—events, people, places, thoughts—are happening in my life?* Look at a portion of your life. It could be what happened today, during the past week, or even a short segment of any time in your life. It could be a situation that inspired great joy or great sorrow. Write out several short phrases or one-word descriptions of what happened, your thoughts, your feelings, which objects or events were involved, your questions for God:

   Object or event:

   My feelings:

   What I think/thought:

   Questions for God:

2. *What can I express to God?* Sometimes we hesitate to really express to God what we are feeling. We either don't seem to have the right words to say or we're afraid to say them. But chances are, whether we want to praise God or tell him our woes, one or more psalms has already expressed a similar thought. By reading a few psalms, you may become more comfortable with the idea of expressing yourself to God.

   a. Praises—read Psalm 8:1–9; 66:1–7; 98:4–9

   b. Laments—read Psalm 94:1–10; 102:1–11; 123

3. *Take it to God!* Using the words you wrote above as a framework, write a psalm to God. If you are uncomfortable writing a psalm, perhaps one of the psalms you read above (or another one you find) already provides the words that express what you want to say to God. If so, meditate on that psalm. Read it, sing it, or memorize it over a period of days. As you write and meditate on the psalm, ask God to reveal himself to you and to continue to teach you more about himself and your relationship with him.

1 min. CLOSING MEDITATION

Let's take a moment to close in prayer.

Dear God, you know everything about us—what we do, what we say, even what we think and how we feel—and still you place your loving hand on us. Wherever we go, you are there. Thank you for allowing us to be who we are with you. Thank you for being willing to accept our doubts, our pain, our fears, and even our despair. Help us to remember that you *want* us to be honest with you about everything. Show us everything in us that offends you, and draw us closer to you. We want to know you better, Lord. Amen.

—Prayer inspired by Psalm 139

NOTES

2. *What can I express to God?* Sometimes we hesitate to really express to God what we are feeling. We either don't seem to have the right words to say or we're afraid to say them. But chances are, whether we want to praise God or tell him our woes, one or more psalms has already expressed a similar thought. By reading a few psalms, you may become more comfortable with the idea of expressing yourself to God.
   a. Praises—read Psalm 8:1–9; 66:1–7; 98:4–9
   b. Laments—read Psalm 94:1–10; 102:1–11; 123

3. *Take it to God!* Using the words you wrote above as a framework, write a psalm to God. If you are uncomfortable writing a psalm, perhaps one of the psalms you read above (or another one you find) already provides the words that express what you want to say to God. If so, meditate on that psalm. Read it, sing it, or memorize it over a period of days. As you write and meditate on the psalm, ask God to reveal himself to you and to continue to teach you more about himself and your relationship with him.

SESSION SIX

Ecclesiastes: The End of Wisdom

BEFORE YOU LEAD

Synopsis

In the video for this session, Philip Yancey describes Ecclesiastes as "the most twenty-first century book in the Bible." This description may surprise some viewers. In fact, Philip himself was surprised to find in Ecclesiastes some of the same themes he had read in modern existentialist literature. "The mysterious, often-ignored book of Ecclesiastes," he writes, "contains every idea and emotion I had encountered in the writers of existential despair."

The anonymous "Teacher," the larger-than-life author of Ecclesiastes, is portrayed as the richest, wisest, and most powerful person of his day. He had the means to satisfy his every need, indeed his every whim. So he pursued all the pleasures the world had to offer and was left with the haunting realization that these pleasures could not satisfy him. Resigned to the futility of life, he cynically concluded that it was *meaningless.*

As he viewed the world around him, the Teacher was jarred by the contradictions of life in this world. Rich people get richer; poor people get poorer. Good people suffer as evil people prosper. Diseases spread. Disasters occur. Tyrants reign. Work hard, and someone else gets the credit. Try to be good, and bad people trample you. Accumulate money, and your spoiled heirs will get it. And no matter what else happens, you and everyone else will eventually die and turn to dust. It all seemed so pointless, so *meaningless.*

Meaningless, the drumbeat of Ecclesiastes, is repeated thirty-five times in this short book. And *meaninglessness* punctuates life in our modern world as well. The more advanced and comfortable we become—the more we try to be like God and live without him—the more our best attempts backfire. We have placed great hope in ourselves, our innovations, our accomplishments. But science and technology cannot banish pain, cure all diseases, or eliminate poverty. More than half the marriages in the most technologically advanced countries end in divorce. Suicide, homelessness, addictions, and violent crime remain with us. In short, as the Teacher learned, whatever humans touch bears a fatal flaw. Our best efforts spell ruin.

"Ecclesiastes," writes Philip Yancey, "sets forth the inevitable consequences of a life without God at the center, and the pitfalls it warns against endanger the believer as much as the pagan." Ecclesiastes has an eerily modern ring to it because human beings (Christians included) still haven't learned its most basic lessons. We can chase the visible world and its pleasures all we want to, but they will not satisfy us. When we set our sights on the visible world only, we will be left wallowing in despair.

Our deliverance, the Teacher of Ecclesiastes concluded, comes from remembering our Creator. Or, in the words of philosopher Ludwig Wittgenstein, "to believe in a God means to see that the facts of this world are not the end of the matter. To believe in God means to see that life has a meaning . . . That this meaning does not lie in it but outside it."

Key Points of This Session

1. Ecclesiastes portrays the inevitable consequences when God is not at the center of human life. Written from the perspective of "the Teacher," who has tried it all and done so in excess, the existential tone of the book matches the despair of our affluent Western culture. In the end, the Teacher freely admits that life doesn't (and can never) make sense apart from God.
2. Ecclesiastes conveys to all of humankind the same message Moses conveyed to the Hebrews in Deuteronomy: Fear God and keep his commandments. It's a tough message for people who have it all. We must be ever cautious that we don't "paper over" our need for God, because the greatest danger we face as humans is to have what we need and forget about him.

Suggested Reading

This session corresponds to Chapter 5 of *The Bible Jesus Read.* You may want to read this chapter in order to deepen your understanding of this material.

Session Outline (51 minutes)

- I. Introduction (5 minutes)
  - A. Welcome
  - B. What's to Come
  - C. Questions to Think About
- II. Video Presentation: "Ecclesiastes: The End of Wisdom" (10 minutes)
- III. Group Discovery (30 minutes)
  - A. Video Highlights (5 minutes)
  - B. Large Group Exploration: Despair in an Age of Prosperity? (10 minutes)
  - C. Small Group Exploration: A Tale of Two Kingdoms (10 minutes)
  - D. Group Discussion (5 minutes)
- IV. Personal Journey (5 minutes)
- V. Closing Meditation (1 minute)

Materials

You'll need a VCR, TV, and Bible. You may also find a whiteboard, flip chart, or overhead projector to be a useful tool in guiding group discussion. View the video prior to leading the session so you are familiar with its main points.

SESSION SIX

Ecclesiastes: The End of Wisdom

The same lesson Job learned in dust and ashes—that we humans cannot figure out life on our own—the Teacher learns in a robe and palace. In the end, the Teacher freely admits that life does not make sense outside of God and will never fully make sense because we are not God. . . . Unless we acknowledge our limits and subject ourselves to God's rule, unless we trust the Giver of all good gifts, we will end up in a state of despair. Ecclesiastes calls us to accept our status as creatures under the dominion of the Creator, something few of us do without a struggle.

—Philip Yancey

5 min. INTRODUCTION

Welcome

Welcome participants to Session 6 of *The Bible Jesus Read* course: "Ecclesiastes: The End of Wisdom."

What's to Come

Today we'll explore the book of Ecclesiastes, which Philip Yancey describes in the video segment as "the most twenty-first century book in the Bible." The anonymous "Teacher," the larger-than-life author of Ecclesiastes, was the richest, wisest, and most powerful person of his day. He had the means to satisfy his every need and whim, and to accomplish anything he set his mind to do. But after he had pursued it all, he concluded that everything in life was meaningless.

This often-ignored book has great relevance to those of us who live in modern, affluent cultures. The meaninglessness and despair that haunted the Teacher of Ecclesiastes punctuate life in our world as well. The more advanced and comfortable we become–the more we try to be like God and live without him–the more our best attempts backfire. The more we have, the more we realize how empty we are. Ecclesiastes forces us to look

NOTES

SESSION SIX

Ecclesiastes: The End of Wisdom

> The same lesson Job learned in dust and ashes—that we humans cannot figure out life on our own—the Teacher learns in a robe and palace. In the end, the Teacher freely admits that life does not make sense outside of God and will never fully make sense because we are not God. . . . Unless we acknowledge our limits and subject ourselves to God's rule, unless we trust the Giver of all good gifts, we will end up in a state of despair. Ecclesiastes calls us to accept our status as creatures under the dominion of the Creator, something few of us do without a struggle.
>
> —Philip Yancey

Questions to Think About

1. When someone mentions the book of Ecclesiastes, what words immediately come to mind? Why?

2. The Bible says that every person needs God, yet some people don't seem to need God at all. They live rich, apparently fulfilling lives without giving God a single thought. In fact, they seem to be doing quite well without him. How can this be?

at reality, to face the inevitable pitfalls and consequences of living life without God at the center of it.

Let's begin by considering a few questions. Please turn to page 87 of your Participant's Guide.

Questions to Think About

Participant's Guide page 87.

As time permits, ask two or more of the following questions and solicit responses from participants.

1. When someone mentions the book of Ecclesiastes, which words immediately come to mind? Why?

Treat this like a word-association exercise. The intent is to "take inventory" of how participants already view the book of Ecclesiastes and what their exposure to it has been.

2. The Bible says that every person needs God, yet some people don't seem to need God at all. They live rich, apparently fulfilling lives without giving God a single thought. In fact, they seem to be doing quite well without him. How can this be?

Responses to this great contradiction will vary. Some people are drawn toward and feel an urgent need for God; others do not. Some people harden their hearts toward God and refuse to turn to him. Some people "need" God only until they get what they want. Others simply cover over their need for God and replace it with whatever this world offers. The more money (security) people have, the less likely they are to recognize their daily need for God and to perceive him as the Giver of all good gifts. When a spiritual ache surfaces, they can simply plug in one more recreation, one more drink, one more new car, or one more sexual fantasy to mask the pain. Point out to the group that many passages in the Old Testament indicate that godless people may triumph in the short term, but one day they will face God and the consequences of their decisions.

3. Some people living in the affluent cultures of the West have every material thing they need and much of what they want, yet are so overwhelmed by despair they don't know why they should go on living. Some of them even end their own lives. What do you think leads prosperous people to despair?

Responses will vary and may include: people long for a deeper meaning in life that possessions cannot provide, people have a spiritual void in their lives, people don't believe they matter, people can't control all the circumstances in their lives, people can't escape their deepest feelings and unmet longings, etc.

NOTES

SESSION SIX

Ecclesiastes: The End of Wisdom

> The same lesson Job learned in dust and ashes—that we humans cannot figure out life on our own—the Teacher learns in a robe and palace. In the end, the Teacher freely admits that life does not make sense outside of God and will never fully make sense because we are not God.... Unless we acknowledge our limits and subject ourselves to God's rule, unless we trust the Giver of all good gifts, we will end up in a state of despair. Ecclesiastes calls us to accept our status as creatures under the dominion of the Creator, something few of us do without a struggle.
>
> —Philip Yancey

Questions to Think About

1. When someone mentions the book of Ecclesiastes, what words immediately come to mind? Why?

2. The Bible says that every person needs God, yet some people don't seem to need God at all. They live rich, apparently fulfilling lives without giving God a single thought. In fact, they seem to be doing quite well without him. How can this be?

3. Some people living in the affluent cultures of the West have every material thing they need and much of what they want, yet are so overwhelmed by despair they don't know why they should go on living. Some of them even end their own lives. What do you think leads prosperous people to despair?

Let's keep these ideas in mind as we view the video. There is space to take notes on page 89.

11 min. VIDEO PRESENTATION: "ECCLESIASTES: THE END OF WISDOM"

Participant's Guide page 89.

Leader's Video Observations

What do you make of Ecclesiastes?

Roots of despair

God goes where he is wanted, to people who know they need him

"Papering over" our need for God during the good times

A time for everything

NOTES

Video Presentation: "Ecclesiastes: The End of Wisdom"

What do you make of Ecclesiastes?

Roots of despair

God goes where he is wanted, to people who know they need him

"Papering over" our need for God during the good times

A time for everything

30 min. GROUP DISCOVERY

If your group has seven or more members, use the Video Highlights with the entire group (5 minutes), then complete the Large Group Exploration (10 minutes), and then break into small groups of three to five people for the Small Group Exploration (10 minutes). Finally, bring everyone together for the closing Group Discussion (5 minutes).

If your group has fewer than seven members, begin with the Video Highlights (5 minutes), then complete both the Large Group Exploration (10 minutes) and the Small Group Exploration (10 minutes) as a group. Wrap up your discovery time with the Group Discussion (5 minutes).

Please turn to page 90 as we discuss some questions related to the video segment we have just seen.

Video Highlights (5 minutes)

Participant's Guide page 90.

As time permits, ask one or more of the following questions, which directly relate to the video the participants have just seen.

1. If we believe that all Scripture is inspired by God, we have to conclude that God wanted Ecclesiastes–a book that focuses on meaninglessness–to be in the Bible. What might be the reasons God wanted the message of Ecclesiastes to be a part of the Bible?

God knows that spiritual poverty leads to a sense of meaninglessness; people at times feel a sense of meaninglessness or despair; God is not afraid to acknowledge our dark moments; God wants us to know that dark moments are not abnormal and that he's willing to walk with us through those times; God knows that no matter how much we have, accomplish, or enjoy, we still need him; God knows that when we cover over our need of him, we're on dangerous ground and may not even know it; etc.

2. Does the theme, "Be careful that you don't forget about God when you grow prosperous and things are going well," sound familiar? Where have you heard it before, and why might we need to hear it again?

This was the theme of Moses' last words to the Hebrews in Deuteronomy—just before they went into the Promised Land. Apparently we still need to hear it because it's been more than 3,000 years since Moses spoke and we haven't learned it yet!

3. In what ways do you agree or disagree with the statement that "times of prosperity are dangerous because we then find it easier to ignore God"? What personal experience can you contribute to our discussion?

NOTES

Video Highlights

1. If we believe that all Scripture is inspired by God, we have to conclude that God wanted Ecclesiastes–a book that focuses on meaninglessness–to be in the Bible. What might be the reasons God wanted the message of Ecclesiastes to be a part of the Bible?

2. Does the theme, "Be careful that you don't forget about God when you grow prosperous and things are going well," sound familiar? Where have you heard it before, and why might we need to hear it again?

3. In what ways do you agree or disagree with the statement that "times of prosperity are dangerous because we then find it easier to ignore God"? What personal experience can you contribute to our discussion?

When our material needs are met, we have a tendency to rely less on God because we think we have something to do with our good fortune. We forget that we are truly dependent on him. We tend to find identity in what we do and have rather than in who we are in God's eyes. We indulge in diversions to keep ourselves from thinking too much about spiritual things. We become self-focused and proud of what we have and can do. But being prosperous is not the whole issue; the issue is the extent to which we rely on, trust in, and obey God no matter how much or little we have.

4. Jesus added a whole new dimension to the meaning of life when he said we gain the world by giving our lives away in service to others, not by accumulating as much as we can. How does this fit with your experience?

Responses will vary, but there are few despairing people who obey God and give themselves in service to others. There are also few people who are focused on accumulating as much as they can in terms of material goods and success who are truly satisfied. What we gain by serving others far outweighs having a longer list of possessions or accomplishments. We also must recognize that living our lives for the benefit of other people is truly a radical idea, especially in a prosperous society.

Perspective

Ecclesiastes sounded its note of doom in an era of unprecedented prosperity and social progress. The ruler over Israel could sense within himself and his nation the failure to sustain the burden. He learned the hard lesson Moses had tried to teach the Israelites centuries before: whatever humans touch will bear a fatal flaw. Good times represent the real danger; our best efforts spell ruin. In short, human beings are not gods, and that realization drove the Teacher to despair.

—Philip Yancey

Now we're ready for the Large Group Exploration part of this session. Please turn to page 92.

Large Group Exploration: Despair in an Age of Prosperity? (10 minutes)

Participant's Guide page 92.

Read the introductory paragraph to the group, then begin discussing the questions that follow.

The "good life" enjoyed by so many people who live in affluent Western cultures is riddled with despair. Many people are trapped in the belief that

NOTES

4. Jesus added a whole new dimension to the meaning of life when he said we gain the world by giving our lives away in service to others, not by accumulating as much as we can. How does this fit with your experience?

Perspective

Ecclesiastes sounded its note of doom in an era of unprecedented prosperity and social progress. The ruler over Israel could sense within himself and his nation the failure to sustain the burden. He learned the hard lesson Moses had tried to teach the Israelites centuries before: whatever humans touch will bear a fatal flaw. Good times represent the real danger; our best efforts spell ruin. In short, human beings are not gods, and that realization drove the Teacher to despair.

—Philip Yancey

Large Group Exploration: Despair in an Age of Prosperity?

The "good life" enjoyed by so many people who live in affluent Western cultures is riddled with despair. Many people are trapped in the belief that life is meaningless, yet they hotly pursue the illusions of meaning anyway! This is the same trap that caught the anonymous Teacher of Ecclesiastes. Let's see what he discovered about life and despair.

1. Despite all the pleasures he tasted and all the things he pursued and accomplished in order to find meaning and purpose, the Teacher in Ecclesiastes found that nothing the world offered added a shred of meaning to his life. Let's look up the following verses and discuss his pursuits and perspective.

What the Teacher Pursued	What the Teacher Discovered
Ecclesiastes 1:13, 16–17:	Ecclesiastes 1:18; 2:16:
Ecclesiastes 2:1–3:	Ecclesiastes 6:7–9; 7:2, 4–6:
Ecclesiastes 2:4–6:	Ecclesiastes 2:17–18:
Ecclesiastes 2:8:	Ecclesiastes 2:21; 5:10–12:
Ecclesiastes 2:9:	Ecclesiastes 3:19–20:

life is meaningless, yet they hotly pursue the illusions of meaning anyway! This is the same trap that caught the anonymous Teacher of Ecclesiastes. Let's see what he discovered about life and despair.

1. Despite all the pleasures he tasted and all the things he pursued and accomplished in order to find meaning and purpose, the Teacher in Ecclesiastes found that nothing the world offered added a shred of meaning to his life. Let's look up the following verses and discuss his pursuits and perspective.

What the Teacher Pursued	What the Teacher Discovered
Ecclesiastes 1:13, 16–17: Wisdom and knowledge	Ecclesiastes 1:18; 2:16: Wisdom and knowledge without God bring sorrow and grief; a wise man is soon forgotten and dies just like a fool
Ecclesiastes 2:1–3: Alcohol and laughter	Ecclesiastes 6:7–9; 7:2, 4–6: Earthly appetite is never satisfied; every person will die eventually; fools place their hearts in the house of pleasure
Ecclesiastes 2:4–6: Wonderful building projects—houses, parks, vineyards, gardens, reservoirs	Ecclesiastes 2:17–18: The projects require work and are left to other people who may be foolish
Ecclesiastes 2:8: Accumulation of wealth and indulgence in sexual pleasure	Ecclesiastes 2:21; 5:10–12: Other people will inherit the possessions; one who loves wealth never has enough and his possessions bring him worries with little benefit
Ecclesiastes 2:9: Fame	Ecclesiastes 3:19–20: Everyone dies; life passes away quickly

Perspective

A despairing book like Ecclesiastes will more likely emerge from a Golden Age. Consider the contrast between Ecclesiastes and Job. They cover many of the same themes—life's unfairness, why suffering exists, why evil people prosper and good ones suffer—but what a difference in tone! Ecclesiastes exudes meaninglessness and futility while Job rings with betrayal, passion, and a cry for justice. Job shakes his fist at God, calls him into account, demands a reply. The Teacher shrugs his shoulders, mumbles, "So what?" and reaches for another goblet of wine. . . . The tone of Ecclesiastes captures precisely the mood of affluent Western countries.

—Philip Yancey

NOTES

Large Group Exploration: Despair in an Age of Prosperity?

The "good life" enjoyed by so many people who live in affluent Western cultures is riddled with despair. Many people are trapped in the belief that life is meaningless, yet they hotly pursue the illusions of meaning anyway! This is the same trap that caught the anonymous Teacher of Ecclesiastes. Let's see what he discovered about life and despair.

1. Despite all the pleasures he tasted and all the things he pursued and accomplished in order to find meaning and purpose, the Teacher in Ecclesiastes found that nothing the world offered added a shred of meaning to his life. Let's look up the following verses and discuss his pursuits and perspective.

What the Teacher Pursued	What the Teacher Discovered
Ecclesiastes 1:13, 16–17:	Ecclesiastes 1:18; 2:16:
Ecclesiastes 2:1–3:	Ecclesiastes 6:7–9; 7:2, 4–6:
Ecclesiastes 2:4–6:	Ecclesiastes 2:17–18:
Ecclesiastes 2:8:	Ecclesiastes 2:21; 5:10–12:
Ecclesiastes 2:9:	Ecclesiastes 3:19–20:

Perspective

A despairing book like Ecclesiastes will more likely emerge from a Golden Age. Consider the contrast between Ecclesiastes and Job. They cover many of the same themes—life's unfairness, why suffering exists, why evil people prosper and good ones suffer—but what a difference in tone! Ecclesiastes exudes meaninglessness and futility while Job rings with betrayal, passion, and a cry for justice. Job shakes his fist at God, calls him into account, demands a reply. The Teacher shrugs his shoulders, mumbles, "So what?" and reaches for another goblet of wine. . . . The tone of Ecclesiastes captures precisely the mood of affluent Western countries.

—Philip Yancey

2. Many of us who live in affluent Western cultures find ourselves walking down a path similar to that of the Teacher of Ecclesiastes. The late Bruno Bettelheim observed, "We should be living in a dawn of great promise. But now that we are freer to enjoy life, we are deeply frustrated in our disappointment that the freedom and comfort, sought with such deep desire, do not give meaning and purpose to our lives." Meaninglessness plagues us just as it did the Teacher. What about life leads us to these feelings of meaninglessness and despair?

3. One of the fascinating aspects of Ecclesiastes is that the Teacher presents his views on the meaninglessness of life in juxtaposition to the

2. Many of us who live in affluent Western cultures find ourselves walking down a path similar to that of the Teacher of Ecclesiastes. The late Bruno Bettelheim observed, "We should be living in a dawn of great promise. But now that we are freer to enjoy life, we are deeply frustrated in our disappointment that the freedom and comfort, sought with such deep desire, do not give meaning and purpose to our lives." Meaninglessness plagues us just as it did the Teacher. What about life leads us to these feelings of meaninglessness and despair?

Encourage participants to think about the roots of meaninglessness. Some examples are the growing disparities between rich and poor, evil people prospering while good people suffer, disasters ruining lives, diseases spreading, young people dying, tyrants ruling, etc.

We want to believe that things make sense, and so often they don't. Prosperity often leads to excess, which may lead to despair. We look to technology to allow us to live well, yet now face carcinogens and nuclear weapons. Families crumble, babies are aborted, teenage suicide rises. The point is, comfort and freedom cannot give meaning and purpose to our lives. Those can only come from a personal relationship with God through Jesus Christ.

3. One of the fascinating aspects of Ecclesiastes is that the Teacher presents his views on the meaninglessness of life in juxtaposition to the reality of God. Surprisingly, his conclusion offers the antidote to despair. What is his conclusion, and what is its relevance to us? (See Ecclesiastes 12:9–14.)

When all is said and done, fearing God and keeping his commandments is most important. One day God will judge each of us for everything we have done. If our focus remains on God, we will have meaning and purpose.

Note: Proverbs offers some practical advice on living a God-focused life. Refer your group to the Did You Know box on Participant's Guide page 94 for some examples of the difference between a human-focused and God-focused perspective.

Please turn to page 95 as we move into the Small Group Exploration part of this session.

Did You Know?

Although the Teacher of Ecclesiastes eventually concluded that the whole duty of humankind is to fear God and keep his commandments, much of the book views daily life from a purely human perspective. In contrast, the writer of Proverbs offers practical wisdom for daily living that is focused more on God. Note the contrasts in the following passages.

NOTES

Perspective

A despairing book like Ecclesiastes will more likely emerge from a Golden Age. Consider the contrast between Ecclesiastes and Job. They cover many of the same themes—life's unfairness, why suffering exists, why evil people prosper and good ones suffer—but what a difference in tone! Ecclesiastes exudes meaninglessness and futility while Job rings with betrayal, passion, and a cry for justice. Job shakes his fist at God, calls him into account, demands a reply. The Teacher shrugs his shoulders, mumbles, "So what?" and reaches for another goblet of wine.... The tone of Ecclesiastes captures precisely the mood of affluent Western countries.

—Philip Yancey

2. Many of us who live in affluent Western cultures find ourselves walking down a path similar to that of the Teacher of Ecclesiastes. The late Bruno Bettelheim observed, "We should be living in a dawn of great promise. But now that we are freer to enjoy life, we are deeply frustrated in our disappointment that the freedom and comfort, sought with such deep desire, do not give meaning and purpose to our lives." Meaninglessness plagues us just as it did the Teacher. What about life leads us to these feelings of meaninglessness and despair?

3. One of the fascinating aspects of Ecclesiastes is that the Teacher presents his views on the meaninglessness of life in juxtaposition to the

reality of God. Surprisingly, his conclusion offers the antidote to despair. What is his conclusion, and what is its relevance to us? (See Ecclesiastes 12:9–14.)

Did You Know?

Although the Teacher of Ecclesiastes eventually concluded that the whole duty of humankind is to fear God and keep his commandments, much of the book views daily life from a purely human perspective. In contrast, the writer of Proverbs offers practical wisdom for daily living that is focused more on God. Note the contrasts in the following passages.

Ecclesiastes on Daily Life	Proverbs on Daily Life
I devoted myself to study and to explore by wisdom all that is done under heaven. What a heavy burden God has laid on men! ... For with much wisdom comes much sorrow; the more knowledge, the more grief (1:13,18).	The LORD gives wisdom, and from his mouth come knowledge and understanding (2:6).
The wise man has eyes in his head, while the fool walks in darkness; but I came to realize that the same fate overtakes them both.... What then do I gain by being wise? (2:14, 15).	Trust in the LORD with all your heart and lean not on your own understanding (3:5).
... The abundance of a rich man permits him no sleep (5:12).	The blessing of the LORD brings wealth, and he adds no trouble to it (10:22).
A feast is made for laughter, and wine makes life merry, but money is the answer for everything (10:19).	Whoever trusts in his riches will fall, but the righteous will thrive like a green leaf (11:28).

Ecclesiastes on Daily Life	Proverbs on Daily Life
I devoted myself to study and to explore by wisdom all that is done under heaven. What a heavy burden God has laid on men! . . . For with much wisdom comes much sorrow; the more knowledge, the more grief (1:13,18).	The LORD gives wisdom, and from his mouth come knowledge and understanding (2:6).
The wise man has eyes in his head, while the fool walks in darkness; but I came to realize that the same fate overtakes them both. . . . What then do I gain by being wise? (2:14, 15).	Trust in the LORD with all your heart and lean not on your own understanding (3:5).
. . . The abundance of a rich man permits him no sleep (5:12).	The blessing of the LORD brings wealth, and he adds no trouble to it (10:22).
A feast is made for laughter, and wine makes life merry, but money is the answer for everything (10:19).	Whoever trusts in his riches will fall, but the righteous will thrive like a green leaf (11:28).

Small Group Exploration: A Tale of Two Kingdoms (10 minutes)

Participant's Guide page 95.

Hovering in the background of Ecclesiastes is the truth that meaningful human life involves more than the visible world we see. Philip Yancey describes the book as presenting "both sides of life on this planet: the promise of pleasures so alluring that we may devote our lives to their pursuit, and then the haunting realization that these pleasures ultimately do not satisfy."

He goes on to explain why the visible world–what we can call the visible kingdom–is not enough: "God's tantalizing world is too big for us. Made for another home, made for eternity, we finally realize that nothing this side of timeless Paradise will quiet the rumors of discontent." So as much as we crave the visible kingdom, our hearts seem to know that we were created to belong in another.

Let's break into groups of three to five and take a few moments to highlight the life and kingdom of King Solomon–the shadow figure of Ecclesiastes–and contrast it with the invisible kingdom of another King.

If you will not be breaking into small groups for the Small Group Exploration, lead the group in a discussion of the following questions.

1. What was the status of the visible kingdom of Israel during Solomon's reign? What illustrates its peace and prosperity? (See 1 Kings 4:25, 34; 10:1–5, 23.)

NOTES

reality of God. Surprisingly, his conclusion offers the antidote to despair. What is his conclusion, and what is its relevance to us? (See Ecclesiastes 12:9–14.)

Did You Know?

Although the Teacher of Ecclesiastes eventually concluded that the whole duty of humankind is to fear God and keep his commandments, much of the book views daily life from a purely human perspective. In contrast, the writer of Proverbs offers practical wisdom for daily living that is focused more on God. Note the contrasts in the following passages.

Ecclesiastes on Daily Life	Proverbs on Daily Life
I devoted myself to study and to explore by wisdom all that is done under heaven. What a heavy burden God has laid on men! ... For with much wisdom comes much sorrow; the more knowledge, the more grief (1:13,18).	The LORD gives wisdom, and from his mouth come knowledge and understanding (2:6).
The wise man has eyes in his head, while the fool walks in darkness; but I came to realize that the same fate overtakes them both.... What then do I gain by being wise? (2:14, 15).	Trust in the LORD with all your heart and lean not on your own understanding (3:5).
... The abundance of a rich man permits him no sleep (5:12).	The blessing of the LORD brings wealth, and he adds no trouble to it (10:22).
A feast is made for laughter, and wine makes life merry, but money is the answer for everything (10:19).	Whoever trusts in his riches will fall, but the righteous will thrive like a green leaf (11:28).

Small Group Exploration: A Tale of Two Kingdoms

Hovering in the background of Ecclesiastes is the truth that meaningful human life involves more than the visible world we see. Philip Yancey describes the book as presenting "both sides of life on this planet: the promise of pleasures so alluring that we may devote our lives to their pursuit, and then the haunting realization that these pleasures ultimately do not satisfy."

He goes on to explain why the visible world—what we can call the visible kingdom—is not enough: "God's tantalizing world is too big for us. Made for another home, made for eternity, we finally realize that nothing this side of timeless Paradise will quiet the rumors of discontent." So as much as we crave the visible kingdom, our hearts seem to know that we were created to belong in another.

Let's break into groups of three to five and take a few moments to highlight the life and kingdom of King Solomon—the shadow figure of Ecclesiastes—and contrast it with the invisible kingdom of another King.

1. What was the status of the visible kingdom of Israel during Solomon's reign? What illustrates its peace and prosperity? (See 1 Kings 4:25, 34; 10:1–5, 23.)

2. What happened to Solomon as time passed? (See 1 Kings 11:1–10.)

There was peace in all of Judah and Israel during Solomon's lifetime. The wars with the Canaanites and others ceased, and people came from all over the world to hear Solomon's wisdom, including the Queen of Sheba. Solomon had more riches and wisdom than all the other kings on earth. God had truly blessed him.

2. What happened to Solomon as time passed? (See 1 Kings 11:1–10.)

He disobeyed God's commands and did not follow God with his whole heart. He had an insatiable sexual appetite and married many pagan wives. He placed pagan idols in Jerusalem and worshiped them.

3. What happened to his kingdom after Solomon's death? (See 1 Kings 12:1–7, 16–17, 26–30.)

The nation split into two completely separate kingdoms (Judah and Israel) and began a downward slide from that day on. It wasn't long before Israel was worshiping the golden calves at Bethel and Dan.

4. Many years later, Jesus came to establish a much different kingdom. Where is this kingdom? (See John 18:36.)

Jesus' kingdom is a heavenly kingdom, an invisible kingdom, a kingdom "not of this world."

Did You Know?

Jesus' perspective on "the good life" differs radically from that of the Teacher of Ecclesiastes. Jesus expressed his perspective to his disciples when he said:

> Blessed are you who are poor, for yours is the kingdom of God. Blessed are you who hunger now, for you will be satisfied. Blessed are you who weep now, for you will laugh. Blessed are you when men hate you, when they exclude you and insult you and reject your name as evil, because of the Son of Man. Rejoice in that day and leap for joy, because great is your reward in heaven. For that is how their fathers treated the prophets. But woe to you who are rich, for you have already received your comfort. Woe to you who are well fed now, for you will go hungry. Woe to you who laugh now, for you will mourn and weep. Woe to you when all men speak well of you, for that is how their fathers treated the false prophets (Luke 6:20–26).

5. What did Jesus reveal about the visible and invisible kingdoms in his parable of the rich fool and in his conversations with the Pharisees? (See Luke 12:16–21; 16:13–15.)

NOTES

Small Group Exploration: A Tale of Two Kingdoms

Hovering in the background of Ecclesiastes is the truth that meaningful human life involves more than the visible world we see. Philip Yancey describes the book as presenting "both sides of life on this planet: the promise of pleasures so alluring that we may devote our lives to their pursuit, and then the haunting realization that these pleasures ultimately do not satisfy."

He goes on to explain why the visible world—what we can call the visible kingdom—is not enough: "God's tantalizing world is too big for us. Made for another home, made for eternity, we finally realize that nothing this side of timeless Paradise will quiet the rumors of discontent." So as much as we crave the visible kingdom, our hearts seem to know that we were created to belong in another.

Let's break into groups of three to five and take a few moments to highlight the life and kingdom of King Solomon—the shadow figure of Ecclesiastes—and contrast it with the invisible kingdom of another King.

1. What was the status of the visible kingdom of Israel during Solomon's reign? What illustrates its peace and prosperity? (See 1 Kings 4:25, 34; 10:1–5, 23.)

2. What happened to Solomon as time passed? (See 1 Kings 11:1–10.)

3. What happened to his kingdom after Solomon's death? (See 1 Kings 12:1–7, 16–17, 26–30.)

4. Many years later, Jesus came to establish a much different kingdom. Where is this kingdom? (See John 18:36.)

Did You Know?

Jesus' perspective on "the good life" differs radically from that of the Teacher of Ecclesiastes. Jesus expressed his perspective to his disciples when he said:

> Blessed are you who are poor, for yours is the kingdom of God. Blessed are you who hunger now, for you will be satisfied. Blessed are you who weep now, for you will laugh. Blessed are you when men hate you, when they exclude you and insult you and reject your name as evil, because of the Son of Man. Rejoice in that day and leap for joy, because great is your reward in heaven. For that is how their fathers treated the prophets. But woe to you who are rich, for you have already received your comfort. Woe to you who are well fed now, for you will go hungry. Woe to you who laugh now, for you will mourn and weep. Woe to you when all men speak well of you, for that is how their fathers treated the false prophets (Luke 6:20–26).

5. What did Jesus reveal about the visible and invisible kingdoms in his parable of the rich fool and in his conversations with the Pharisees? (See Luke 12:16–21; 16:13–15.)

6. How is what Jesus said to his disciples similar to what the Teacher in Ecclesiastes said at the end of his book? (See Matthew 16:24–27; Ecclesiastes 12:13–14.)

Perspective

The account of decadence by the richest, wisest, most talented person in the world serves as a perfect allegory for what can happen when we lose sight of the Giver whose good gifts we enjoy. Pleasure represents a great good but also a grave danger. If we start chasing pleasure as an end in itself, along the way we may lose sight of the One who gave us such good gifts as sexual drive, taste buds, and the capacity to appreciate beauty. In that event, as Ecclesiastes tells it, a wholesale devotion to pleasure will paradoxically lead to a state of utter despair.

—Philip Yancey

The rich fool was going to take the path Solomon took—to simply enjoy the benefits of this world and ignore the invisible spiritual world. By what happened after the rich man's death, God made it clear that people must pay attention to the invisible world. In his comments to the Pharisees, Jesus likewise reminded us of the difference between loving and pursuing the visible world and loving and pursuing God and his invisible kingdom.

6. How is what Jesus said to his disciples similar to what the Teacher in Ecclesiastes said at the end of his book? (See Matthew 16:24–27; Ecclesiastes 12:13–14.)

Jesus asked what good it would be to obtain the entire world (the visible kingdom) and yet lose one's soul (God's invisible kingdom). He reinforced the fact that God will judge every person according to what he or she has done in relationship to those kingdoms. The Teacher's conclusion is similar: don't forget to obey God (to live according to the invisible kingdom) while you go about life (in the visible kingdom). He also reinforced God's coming judgment.

Perspective

The account of decadence by the richest, wisest, most talented person in the world serves as a perfect allegory for what can happen when we lose sight of the Giver whose good gifts we enjoy. Pleasure represents a great good but also a grave danger. If we start chasing pleasure as an end in itself, along the way we may lose sight of the One who gave us such good gifts as sexual drive, taste buds, and the capacity to appreciate beauty. In that event, as Ecclesiastes tells it, a wholesale devotion to pleasure will paradoxically lead to a state of utter despair.

—Philip Yancey

If you have divided into small groups, let participants know when there is 1 minute remaining.

Give participants a moment to transition from their small group discussions. If time allows, or if you have assigned each group a specific question, have representatives from the groups share their key ideas.

Now let's wrap up our Group Discovery time. Please turn to page 98.

Group Discussion (5 minutes)

Participant's Guide page 98.

Use one or more of the following questions to encourage participants to share their observations with the entire group.

1. In what ways have your opinions of Ecclesiastes changed as a result of this session?

NOTES

5. What did Jesus reveal about the visible and invisible kingdoms in his parable of the rich fool and in his conversations with the Pharisees? (See Luke 12:16–21; 16:13–15.)

6. How is what Jesus said to his disciples similar to what the Teacher in Ecclesiastes said at the end of his book? (See Matthew 16:24–27; Ecclesiastes 12:13–14.)

Perspective

The account of decadence by the richest, wisest, most talented person in the world serves as a perfect allegory for what can happen when we lose sight of the Giver whose good gifts we enjoy. Pleasure represents a great good but also a grave danger. If we start chasing pleasure as an end in itself, along the way we may lose sight of the One who gave us such good gifts as sexual drive, taste buds, and the capacity to appreciate beauty. In that event, as Ecclesiastes tells it, a wholesale devotion to pleasure will paradoxically lead to a state of utter despair.

—Philip Yancey

Group Discussion

1. In what ways have your opinions of Ecclesiastes changed as a result of this session?

2. Philip Yancey quotes J. I. Packer as calling Ecclesiastes the "one book in Scripture that is expressly designed to turn us into realists." Why do you think he came to this conclusion, and in what ways do you agree or disagree with it?

3. Name some people–personal acquaintances, Bible characters, notable people from history, or well-known contemporary people–who seem to have found peace and meaning in life. What do you think gives them peace and meaning?

2. Philip Yancey quotes J. I. Packer as calling Ecclesiastes the "one book in Scripture that is expressly designed to turn us into realists." Why do you think he came to this conclusion, and in what ways do you agree or disagree with it?

3. Name some people—personal acquaintances, Bible characters, notable people from history, or well-known contemporary people—who seem to have found peace and meaning in life. What do you think gives them peace and meaning?

Now it's time for each of us to consider on a personal level what we've been discussing and thinking about. Please turn to page 99.

6 min. PERSONAL JOURNEY: TO BEGIN NOW

Participant's Guide page 99.

Ecclesiastes portrays the inevitable consequences when God is not at the center of human life. Written from the perspective of the Teacher, who has tried it all and done so in excess, the existential tone of the book matches the despair of our affluent Western culture. Take some time now by yourself to consider what you have discovered in this session and how it applies to your life.

1. In the end, the Teacher freely admits that life doesn't (and can never) make sense apart from God. Describe an experience that might have led you to the realization that life doesn't make sense or is unfair.

   a. What was your emotional response to that realization?

   b. If you were to honestly share your thoughts and feelings about the meaning of life with God and heard his answer, how do you think your perspective might change?

2. Ecclesiastes conveys to all of humankind the same message Moses conveyed to the Hebrews in Deuteronomy: Fear God and keep his commandments. It's a tough message for people who have it all. We must be ever cautious that we don't "paper over" our need for God, because the greatest danger we face as humans is to have what we need and forget about him.

   a. In what ways are you tempted to create your own little "kingdom"—having pride in what you have done and plan to do—apart from God?

   b. If you were to take to heart the Teacher's advice, "Fear God and keep his commandments," what difference do you think it would make in your life? In the lives of people around you?

Let participants know when there is 1 minute remaining. Remind participants that they may want to continue their journey by completing the additional exercise on page 101 of their Participant's Guide before the next session.

NOTES

Group Discussion

1. In what ways have your opinions of Ecclesiastes changed as a result of this session?

2. Philip Yancey quotes J. I. Packer as calling Ecclesiastes the "one book in Scripture that is expressly designed to turn us into realists." Why do you think he came to this conclusion, and in what ways do you agree or disagree with it?

3. Name some people—personal acquaintances, Bible characters, notable people from history, or well-known contemporary people—who seem to have found peace and meaning in life. What do you think gives them peace and meaning?

Personal Journey: To Begin Now

Ecclesiastes portrays the inevitable consequences when God is not at the center of human life. Written from the perspective of the Teacher, who has tried it all and done so in excess, the existential tone of the book matches the despair of our affluent Western culture. Take some time now by yourself to consider what you have discovered in this session and how it applies to your life.

1. In the end, the Teacher freely admits that life doesn't (and can never) make sense apart from God. Describe an experience that might have led you to the realization that life doesn't make sense or is unfair.
   a. What was your emotional response to that realization?

   b. If you were to honestly share your thoughts and feelings about the meaning of life with God and heard his answer, how do you think your perspective might change?

2. Ecclesiastes conveys to all of humankind the same message Moses conveyed to the Hebrews in Deuteronomy: Fear God and keep his commandments. It's a tough message for people who have it all. We must be ever cautious that we don't "paper over" our need for God, because the greatest danger we face as humans is to have what we need and forget about him.
   a. In what ways are you tempted to create your own little "kingdom"—having pride in what you have done and plan to do—apart from God?

   b. If you were to take to heart the Teacher's advice, "Fear God and keep his commandments," what difference do you think it would make in your life? In the lives of people around you?

PERSONAL JOURNEY: TO DO BETWEEN SESSIONS

As a result of his study, Philip Yancey writes, "I have come to see Ecclesiastes not as a mistake, nor as a contrived form of reverse apologetics, rather as a profound reminder of the limits of being human. Ecclesiastes sets forth the inevitable consequences of a life without God at the center, and the pitfalls it warns against endanger the believer as much as the pagan."

In light of this quote, before the next session, set aside time away from distractions to do the following exercise.

1. What limits of being human do you have a hard time facing?
2. In what ways are you depending on the visible world to "paper over" your human limits?
3. In what ways are you trying to find meaning in what this world has to offer?
4. What are the pitfalls and consequences of living without God in those areas of your life?
5. Take some time this week to read and meditate on Chapters 2 and 3 of Ecclesiastes, particularly verses 2:10–11; 17–26; 3:9–15. Note the difference in perspective between living in light of the visible world only as opposed to living in light of God's perspective. Ask God to reveal to you the ways you are searching for meaning apart from him.

1 min. CLOSING MEDITATION

Let's take a moment to close in prayer.

Dear God, thank you for the meaning and purpose you bring to life. We don't have to search for them in the pleasures of this world. We already know where that leads. Nor do we have to live in despair like so many people today. Without you we truly are poor, needy, and empty. Please guard our lives and fill us with your Spirit. Draw us closer to you and bring us joy. You are forgiving and good, abounding in love to every person who calls to you. Teach us to walk in your ways. Give us undivided hearts that yearn for you. Great is your love toward us. Help us to remember that whenever we face a time when we feel lost and think that life has no meaning, you are with us—and you are always willing to provide hope, wisdom, and guidance to those who seek you. Amen.

—Prayer inspired by Psalm 86

NOTES

Personal Journey: To Do between Sessions

As a result of his study, Philip Yancey writes, "I have come to see Ecclesiastes not as a mistake, nor as a contrived form of reverse apologetics, rather as a profound reminder of the limits of being human. Ecclesiastes sets forth the inevitable consequences of a life without God at the center, and the pitfalls it warns against endanger the believer as much as the pagan."

1. What limits of being human do you have a hard time facing?

2. In what ways are you depending on the visible world to "paper over" your human limits?

3. In what ways are you trying to find meaning in what this world has to offer?

4. What are the pitfalls and consequences of living without God in those areas of your life?

5. Take some time this week to read and meditate on Chapters 2 and 3 of Ecclesiastes, particularly verses 2:10–11; 17–26; 3:9–15. Note the difference in perspective between living in light of the visible world only as opposed to living in light of God's perspective. Ask God to reveal to you the ways you are searching for meaning apart from him.

SESSION SEVEN

The Prophets: God Talks Back

BEFORE YOU LEAD

Synopsis

The seventeen books of the prophets make up about one-fifth of the Bible, but most people rarely read them. Yet the prophets offer something very unique. Throughout much of the Old Testament people ask questions of God, but in the prophets *God talks back!*

In this session we will consider the books of the prophets, which provide the Bible's most complete and dramatic revelation of God's personality. Guided by Philip Yancey, we will discover the outstanding truth that he learned about God from the prophets: God is personal and cares about every human being.

Philip Yancey admits that these books are not easy to understand. Complaints that they are "weird, confusing, and all sound alike"—do not easily disappear. There are, however, some guiding concepts that help make these mysterious books a bit more approachable:

- The prophetic books were not written as books. They are collections of speeches given to different groups at different times. So it helps to understand the context—place, time frame, audience, current circumstances—during which each was written.
- The prophetic books, more than any others, reveal how God thinks and what he feels.
- The prophets reveal as much about who God is as they do about future events.
- The prophets present God's cosmic viewpoint: the past, the present, the future are all presented from his timeless perspective—a perspective we don't have.
- The prophets don't bother to tell us whether events they speak of will occur the next day or in three thousand years.

The prophets themselves were extremists who would do just about anything to get people's attention. They sounded the alarm over and over again, inviting people to turn back to God. Theirs wasn't an easy job. Isaiah, for example, spent years in the political limelight advising the kings of Judah. When they refused to listen to God's warnings, he stripped off his clothes and walked naked around Jerusalem for three years, hoping that deaf ears would hear (and that blind eyes wouldn't see him!). To get his point across, Jeremiah, who sometimes couldn't wait to speak God's words and at other times wanted to do anything but pronounce gloom and doom, staggered under the weight of an ox yoke.

The startling imagery and mythic visions of the prophets seem strange to us because we lack the capacity to see the world through God's timeless, transcendent perspective. But at the same time, the prophets understood how people think, and their words penetrate our hearts and minds. The prophets' message is no less significant for us today than it was for the original audience. God doesn't run the world the way we might run it, but how we live in relationship to God makes a crucial difference. The prophets continually remind us that the world will eventually become what God wants it to become, and our challenge is to live in that hope no matter what events transpire.

Key Points of This Session

1. Ironically, the seventeen most unread books of the Bible are the same books that give us the most complete picture of God's personality. With a passion that borders on the bizarre, the prophets proclaim to the human race that we matter to God. Over and over again, their urgent messages ring out to reveal a personal God who cares about every human being, who longs to be in relationship with us, and who–above all–loves us.
2. The startling actions and mythic visions of the prophets seem strange to us because the prophets are revealing to mortal humans a glimpse of God's cosmic viewpoint. The prophets seek to open our eyes to the world as God sees it, and that viewpoint is, at best, difficult for us to grasp. Their messages transcend time, speaking to the present as well as to the future. If we will listen, we will gain a vision of what God is ultimately doing in the world and will receive hope to endure the challenges of the present.

Suggested Reading

This session corresponds to Chapter 6 of *The Bible Jesus Read.* You may want to read this chapter in order to deepen your understanding of this material.

Session Outline (52 minutes)

I. Introduction (5 minutes)
   A. Welcome
   B. What's to Come
   C. Questions to Think About
II. Video Presentation: "The Prophets: God Talks Back" (11 minutes)
III. Group Discovery (30 minutes)
   A. Video Highlights (5 minutes)
   B. Large Group Exploration: Getting to Know the God Who Loves Us (10 minutes)
   C. Small Group Exploration: A Fresh Look at the Prophets (10 minutes)
   D. Group Discussion (5 minutes)
IV. Personal Journey (5 minutes)
V. Closing Meditation (1 minute)

Materials

You'll need a VCR, TV, and Bible. You may also find a whiteboard, flip chart, or overhead projector to be a useful tool in guiding group discussion. View the video prior to leading the session so you are familiar with its main points.

SESSION SEVEN

The Prophets: God Talks Back

Why read the prophets? There is one compelling reason: to get to know God. The prophets are the Bible's most forceful revelation of God's personality. . . . One who reads the prophets encounters not an impassible, distant deity but an actual Person, a God as passionate as any person you have met. God feels delight, and frustration, and anger. He weeps and moans with pain. . . . The prophets proclaim loud and clear how God feels: he loves us.

—Philip Yancey

5 min. INTRODUCTION

Welcome

Welcome participants to Session 7 of *The Bible Jesus Read* course: "The Prophets: God Talks Back."

What's to Come

Today we're going to consider the books of the Old Testament prophets. Compared to other books of the Bible, few people read these books, yet they offer incredible insights into God's personality. These are the books in which God talks back to us, and they overflow with messages of his love for each of us.

Of course, it's no secret that these books are also difficult to understand. They seem strange to us because they portray the world as God sees it—timeless and transcendent—and we don't have the capacity to see his cosmic view. Nevertheless, these books have messages for us. If we will pay attention, we will gain a vision of what God is ultimately doing in the world and will gain hope to endure the challenges we face in life.

Let's begin by considering a few questions. Please turn to page 103 of your Participant's Guide.

NOTES

SESSION SEVEN

The Prophets: God Talks Back

> Why read the prophets? There is one compelling reason: to get to know God. The prophets are the Bible's most forceful revelation of God's personality. . . . One who reads the prophets encounters not an impassible, distant deity but an actual Person, a God as passionate as any person you have met. God feels delight, and frustration, and anger. He weeps and moans with pain. . . . The prophets proclaim loud and clear how God feels: he loves us.
>
> —Philip Yancey

Questions to Think About

1. When you think of the prophetic books of the Bible such as Amos, Obadiah, Jeremiah, Daniel, Isaiah, and Habakkuk, which words, images, and feelings come to mind?

2. From what you know of the Bible, what do you think God is like? In what ways does your understanding of God as portrayed in the prophets differ from your understanding of him as presented elsewhere in Scripture?

103

Questions to Think About

Participant's Guide page 103.

As time permits, ask two or more of the following questions and solicit responses from the participants.

1. When you think of the prophetic books of the Bible such as Amos, Obadiah, Jeremiah, Daniel, Isaiah, and Habakkuk, which words, images, and feelings come to mind?

View this as a type of word-association exercise that helps people identify their existing perceptions (and what may be obstacles to understanding the prophets). Some participants may consider these books to be confusing or boring. Some may have gained significant insights and encouragement from these books. Some may be shocked by what God had his prophets do in order to communicate his message. Others may have been impressed by fantastic, bigger-than-life beasts and been curious about their meaning. Others may be fed up with what they think are repetitive and incomprehensible books. Still others may think of the *Left Behind* series, which in the minds of many readers has become a focal point of prophecy.

2. From what you know of the Bible, what do you think God is like? In what ways does your understanding of God as portrayed in the prophets differ from your understanding of him as presented elsewhere in Scripture?

The intent of this question is to identify existing perceptions, which may include: God is love, God hates sin, God is all-knowing, God is eternal, God punishes, God is compassionate and forgiving. If no one mentions that God is personal—that he loves and cares about each of us—take time to mention this important characteristic of God, which is emphasized over and over again in the Bible's prophetic books. The intent is also to see if participants already recognize a difference between the portrayal of God in the prophets as opposed to his portrayal in other biblical books.

3. What did the Old Testament prophets actually do?

Most people think of prophets in the limited sense of foretelling the future. See if you can broaden the perspective to a prophet being a "seer," one who sees the bigger picture of what is taking place. Help participants realize that the prophets spoke for God, that one of their objectives was to turn people's hearts back to God, and that their messages are still relevant today.

4. If you knew that something terrible was going to happen to everybody within twenty miles of your home a week from today unless everyone repented of their sin and turned to God, what would you do? How far would you go to tell your message? What might people think of you for doing it?

NOTES

SESSION SEVEN

The Prophets: God Talks Back

> Why read the prophets? There is one compelling reason: to get to know God. The prophets are the Bible's most forceful revelation of God's personality. . . . One who reads the prophets encounters not an impassible, distant deity but an actual Person, a God as passionate as any person you have met. God feels delight, and frustration, and anger. He weeps and moans with pain. . . . The prophets proclaim loud and clear how God feels: he loves us.
>
> —Philip Yancey

Questions to Think About

1. When you think of the prophetic books of the Bible such as Amos, Obadiah, Jeremiah, Daniel, Isaiah, and Habakkuk, which words, images, and feelings come to mind?

2. From what you know of the Bible, what do you think God is like? In what ways does your understanding of God as portrayed in the prophets differ from your understanding of him as presented elsewhere in Scripture?

3. What did the Old Testament prophets actually do?

4. If you knew that something terrible was going to happen to everybody within twenty miles of your home a week from today unless everyone repented of their sin and turned to God, what would you do? How far would you go to tell your message? What might people think of you for doing it?

Most participants will express that they would do everything they could to get people's attention. This might include going on the airwaves, going door to door, putting up signs, talking with church and community leaders, etc. Some participants may even mention extreme measures. Participants will probably agree that some people might listen, others might become angry, and some might laugh or think you are crazy.

Let's keep these ideas in mind as we view the video. There is space to take notes on page 105.

11 min. VIDEO PRESENTATION: "THE PROPHETS: GOD TALKS BACK"

Participant's Guide page 105.

Leader's Video Observations

God talks back: his personality revealed

Understanding the prophets

Crazy guys doing whatever it takes to make the point

Prophets in context

Making the prophets personal

NOTES

Video Presentation: "The Prophets: God Talks Back"

God talks back: his personality revealed

Understanding the prophets

Crazy guys doing whatever it takes to make the point

Prophets in context

Making the prophets personal

30 min. GROUP DISCOVERY

If your group has seven or more members, use the Video Highlights with the entire group (5 minutes), then complete the Large Group Exploration (10 minutes), and then break into small groups of three to five people for the Small Group Exploration (10 minutes). Finally, bring everyone together for the closing Group Discussion (5 minutes).

If your group has fewer than seven members, begin with the Video Highlights (5 minutes), then complete both the Large Group Exploration (10 minutes) and the Small Group Exploration (10 minutes) as a group. Wrap up your discovery time with the Group Discussion (5 minutes).

Please turn to page 106 as we discuss some questions related to the video segment we have just seen.

Video Highlights (5 minutes)

Participant's Guide page 106.

As time permits, ask one or more of the following questions, which directly relate to the video the participants have just seen.

1. One of the things that helped open up the books of the prophets for Philip Yancey was to view them more as a revelation of God's personality than a revelation of history or the future. In what ways might that change in approach affect our ability to appreciate these books?

To be able to read these books and see what they reveal about the God who loves us certainly lightens the load. Trying to figure out what prophecies mean is truly intimidating, even for the best Bible scholars. But reading the books in order to get to know God more intimately is possible and even inviting.

2. When you consider the lengths to which the prophets went in order to communicate God's message, what would have been your response if God had chosen you to be a prophet and given you an important message to communicate to your society?

Some participants would have asked God to use somebody else, some would have given up, others would have done much more to attract attention, and still others would have been horrified to even consider using the bizarre tactics of the prophets. The point is to help participants realize what an uphill battle the prophets faced and how desperately they felt the need to communicate God's messages.

3. Describe a time in your reading of the prophets when you have experienced a point of strong identity with a prophet, particularly his feelings or perceptions. What about a time when certain words "jumped off the page" and touched a deep need in your heart?

NOTES

106 The Bible Jesus Read Participant's Guide

Video Highlights

1. One of the things that helped open up the books of the prophets for Philip Yancey was to view them more as a revelation of God's personality than a revelation of history or the future. In what ways might that change in approach affect our ability to appreciate these books?

2. When you consider the lengths to which the prophets went in order to communicate God's message, what would have been your response if God had chosen you to be a prophet and given you an important message to communicate to your society?

3. Describe a time in your reading of the prophets when you have experienced a point of strong identity with a prophet, particularly his feelings or perceptions. What about a time when certain words "jumped off the page" and touched a deep need in your heart?

Philip Yancey shared these experiences in the latter part of the video. Such experiences help us realize the personal value of the prophets to us. Encourage participants to share their similar experiences. If no one answers, be prepared to share your experiences.

Did You Know?

I found the prophets to be the most "modern" writers imaginable. In chapter after chapter they deal with the very same themes that hang like a cloud over our century: the silence of God, economic disparity, injustice, war, the seeming sovereignty of evil, the unrelieved suffering that afflicts our world. These, the same themes that surface periodically in Job, Psalms, Ecclesiastes, and even Deuteronomy, the prophets bring into sharp focus, as if examining them under a microscope.

—Philip Yancey

Now we're ready for the Large Group Exploration part of this session. Please turn to page 108.

Large Group Exploration: Getting to Know the God Who Loves Us (10 minutes)

Participant's Guide page 108.

Read the introductory paragraph to the group, then begin discussing the questions that follow.

The prophets, although they may seem terribly foreign and distant to us, reveal amazingly intimate exchanges between God and his people. Faced with people who weren't listening to God, the prophets experienced the anguish of seeing God seemingly pulling farther and farther away from his creation. They challenged him to miraculously display his power as he did in the days of Moses. They asked him tough questions: "Why is there so much poverty?" "Why don't you *speak* and *act* now?" In response to their questions, God answered! He revealed his innermost thoughts—his passion, his delight, his anger, and his frustration. Most important, he revealed how very much we matter to him.

Let's consider a few passages from the prophets that will help us become better acquainted with the God who loves us.

1. The prophets expressed themselves honestly—sometimes brutally so—to God. Let's see just how strongly they expressed themselves. (See Isaiah 64:7, 10–12; Jeremiah 14:8–9; Habakkuk 1:2–4.)

NOTES

Did You Know?

I found the prophets to be the most "modern" writers imaginable. In chapter after chapter they deal with the very same themes that hang like a cloud over our century: the silence of God, economic disparity, injustice, war, the seeming sovereignty of evil, the unrelieved suffering that afflicts our world. These, the same themes that surface periodically in Job, Psalms, Ecclesiastes, and even Deuteronomy, the prophets bring into sharp focus, as if examining them under a microscope.

—Philip Yancey

Large Group Exploration: Getting to Know the God Who Loves Us

The prophets, although they may seem terribly foreign and distant to us, reveal amazingly intimate exchanges between God and his people. Faced with people who weren't listening to God, the prophets experienced the anguish of seeing God seemingly pulling farther and farther away from his creation. They challenged him to miraculously display his power as he did in the days of Moses. They asked him tough questions: "Why is there so much poverty?" "Why don't you *speak* and *act* now?" In response to their questions, God answered! He revealed his innermost thoughts—his passion, his delight, his anger, and his frustration. Most important, he revealed how very much we matter to him.

Let's consider a few passages from the prophets that will help us become better acquainted with the God who loves us.

1. The prophets expressed themselves honestly—sometimes brutally so—to God. Let's see just how strongly they expressed themselves. (See Isaiah 64:7, 10–12; Jeremiah 14:8–9; Habakkuk 1:2–4.)

2. Sometimes God responds in anger when we show disregard for him. At other times he responds more like a wounded lover, weeping and moaning with pain. Let's look at a sampling of his responses in the books of the prophets. What do we learn about God through them?

Isaiah said that God hides himself. Jeremiah asked God why he was like a visitor to his people, like a man surprised by circumstances and a warrior powerless to save anyone. Habakkuk complained that God wasn't listening to his calls for help, that God tolerated injustice and evil, that the world was full of destruction and violence and conflict, that justice didn't prevail, and that wicked people were overwhelming the righteous.

2. Sometimes God responds in anger when we show disregard for him. At other times he responds more like a wounded lover, weeping and moaning with pain. Let's look at a sampling of his responses in the books of the prophets. What do we learn about God through them?

Scripture	**God's Response**
Habakkuk 1:2–7	In response to Habakkuk's complaint against injustice, God said he would do something unbelievable—utterly amazing—to get the attention of his people. He would send the fearsome Babylonians to punish them.
Isaiah 51:4, 11	God spoke to his people in a very personal way, calling them "my people" and "my nation." He implored them to listen. And despite their unfaithfulness and sin, he still envisioned them at their best—safe in his city, joyful and singing.
Jeremiah 3:12–15	God expressed mercy, love, forgiveness, compassion, and tenderness as he literally begged his people to return to him so that he could show his love and faithfulness to them. Calling himself their "husband," he longed to nurture them, guide them, and share his heart with them.
Zephaniah 3:17	God takes great delight in his people. His heart overflowed with tenderness as he described quieting them with his love and rejoicing over them with singing!
Hosea 11:8–10	This is a passionate declaration of God's love, of how his compassion overruled his legitimate anger and how he longed to care for his errant people.

3. The prophets reveal how very much God's people matter to him. Read Jeremiah 31:3–14. What evidence do we find in this passage that we matter to God?

God's love is everlasting; he would rebuild them following their destruction; he would bring them back; he would lead them; they were his family, he scattered them for their good; he watched over them like a shepherd; he paid their ransom; he would turn their bad fortune into good. He did all of this and more because they mattered!

NOTES

Large Group Exploration: Getting to Know the God Who Loves Us

The prophets, although they may seem terribly foreign and distant to us, reveal amazingly intimate exchanges between God and his people. Faced with people who weren't listening to God, the prophets experienced the anguish of seeing God seemingly pulling farther and farther away from his creation. They challenged him to miraculously display his power as he did in the days of Moses. They asked him tough questions: "Why is there so much poverty?" "Why don't you *speak* and *act* now?" In response to their questions, God answered! He revealed his innermost thoughts—his passion, his delight, his anger, and his frustration. Most important, he revealed how very much we matter to him.

Let's consider a few passages from the prophets that will help us become better acquainted with the God who loves us.

1. The prophets expressed themselves honestly—sometimes brutally so—to God. Let's see just how strongly they expressed themselves. (See Isaiah 64:7, 10–12; Jeremiah 14:8–9; Habakkuk 1:2–4.)

2. Sometimes God responds in anger when we show disregard for him. At other times he responds more like a wounded lover, weeping and moaning with pain. Let's look at a sampling of his responses in the books of the prophets. What do we learn about God through them?

Scripture	God's Response
Habakkuk 1:2–7	
Isaiah 51:4, 11	
Jeremiah 3:12–15	
Zephaniah 3:17	
Hosea 11:8–10	

3. The prophets reveal how very much God's people matter to him. Read Jeremiah 31:3–14. What evidence do we find in this passage that we matter to God?

Did You Know?

One important message shines through with great force: God passionately desires his people. Above all else, the prophets repeat the constant refrain of the Old Testament, that we *matter* to God.

—Philip Yancey

Did You Know?

One important message shines through with great force: God passionately desires his people. Above all else, the prophets repeat the constant refrain of the Old Testament, that we *matter* to God.

—Philip Yancey

Please turn to page 110 as we move into the Small Group Exploration part of this session.

Small Group Exploration: A Fresh Look at the Prophets (10 minutes)

Participant's Guide page 110.

We're going to do something a bit different in our small groups today. After breaking into groups of three to five, have someone in your group read the Scripture passage listed. Then discuss the questions that follow, using the perspectives we have gained from this session to make these intimidating books more approachable.

If you will not be breaking into small groups for the Small Group Exploration, lead the group in a discussion of the following questions.

Read Micah 4:1–5:2.

1. In *The Bible Jesus Read,* Philip Yancey provides some tips for reading the prophets. He categorizes the prophet's insights roughly into three categories, which will help you overcome barriers you may have against reading the prophets, and also help you to discover the books' essential messages: (1) *Now prophecies* relate primarily to situations in each prophet's own day; (2) *Later prophecies* are well removed from each prophet's own time but were later fulfilled in history; and (3) *Much later prophecies* seem still to lie in the future.

   Which *now, later,* or *much later* prophecies can you identify in Micah 4:1–5:2?

2. "As 'seers,' the prophets have insight into God's perspective," Philip Yancey explains. "Keep in mind that the prophets didn't tell us when the predicted events will happen and sometimes combine near and distant predictions in the same paragraph.... Sequence is a minor issue for the God who lives outside the constraints of time."

   What from this passage indicates that sequence was a minor issue for the prophet?

3. Sometimes the books of the prophets permit us to glimpse into the cosmic view of history–the history behind the history. In Daniel 10, for example, an angel explained to Daniel that "the prince of the Persian kingdom" had prevented him from answering Daniel's prayer for

NOTES

Scripture	God's Response
Habakkuk 1:2–7	
Isaiah 51:4, 11	
Jeremiah 3:12–15	
Zephaniah 3:17	
Hosea 11:8–10	

3. The prophets reveal how very much God's people matter to him. Read Jeremiah 31:3–14. What evidence do we find in this passage that we matter to God?

Did You Know?

One important message shines through with great force: God passionately desires his people. Above all else, the prophets repeat the constant refrain of the Old Testament, that we *matter* to God.
—Philip Yancey

Small Group Exploration: A Fresh Look at the Prophets

We're going to do something a bit different in our small groups today. After breaking into groups of three to five, have someone in your group read the Scripture passage listed. Then discuss the questions that follow, using the perspectives we have gained from this session to make these intimidating books more approachable.

Read Micah 4:1–5:2.

1. In *The Bible Jesus Read,* Philip Yancey provides some tips for reading the prophets. He categorizes the prophet's insights roughly into three categories, which will help you overcome barriers you may have against reading the prophets, and also help you to discover the books' essential messages: (1) *Now prophecies* relate primarily to situations in each prophet's own day; (2) *Later prophecies* are well removed from each prophet's own time but were later fulfilled in history; and (3) *Much later prophecies* seem still to lie in the future.
   Which *now, later,* or *much later* prophecies can you identify in Micah 4:1–5:2?

2. "As 'seers,' the prophets have insight into God's perspective," Philip Yancey explains. "Keep in mind that the prophets didn't tell us when the predicted events will happen and sometimes combine near and distant predictions in the same paragraph.... Sequence is a minor issue for the God who lives outside the constraints of time."
   What from this passage indicates that sequence was a minor issue for the prophet?

3. Sometimes the books of the prophets permit us to glimpse into the cosmic view of history—the history behind the history. In Daniel 10, for example, an angel explained to Daniel that "the prince of the Persian kingdom" had prevented him from answering Daniel's prayer for twenty-one days. Finally, reinforcements arrived, and Michael—a chief angel—helped him break through the opposition. So Daniel played a decisive role in the warfare between cosmic forces of good and evil, though much of the action was beyond his range of vision.
   Which portions of this passage are indicative of God's cosmic view—a view that we have a hard time grasping?

twenty-one days. Finally, reinforcements arrived, and Michael—a chief angel—helped him break through the opposition. So Daniel played a decisive role in the warfare between cosmic forces of good and evil, though much of the action was beyond his range of vision.

Which portions of this passage are indicative of God's cosmic view—a view that we have a hard time grasping?

4. In what ways do you see God's personality—his thoughts, feelings, character—revealed through this passage?

5. Philip Yancey notes that "the prophets call us beyond the fears and grim reality of present history to the view of all eternity, to a time when God's reign will fill the earth with light and truth."

   Which portion(s) of this passage give you a glimpse of God's ultimate viewpoint and give you hope to endure the challenges of your life?

Perspective

The prophets . . . render God's point of view. God granted them (and, through them, us) the extraordinary vision to see past this world, dominated as it is by great powers and larger-than-life tyrants, to a different level of reality. We get a glimpse, a mere glimpse, of history from God's viewpoint. No wonder the prophets seem strange: we lack the capacity for seeing the world from the vantage point of timelessness.

—Philip Yancey

If you have divided into small groups, let participants know when there is 1 minute remaining.

Give participants a moment to transition from their small group discussions. If time allows, or if you have assigned each group a specific question, have representatives from the groups share their key ideas.

Now let's wrap up our Group Discovery time. Please turn to page 113.

Group Discussion (5 minutes)

Participant's Guide page 113.

Use one or more of the following questions to encourage participants to share their observations with the entire group.

1. Would one or two of you please share some highlights of your small group discussion with the whole group?

2. The following portion of *The Bible Jesus Read* captures beautifully the importance of the prophets' message for us today. Listen carefully:

NOTES

2. "As 'seers,' the prophets have insight into God's perspective," Philip Yancey explains. "Keep in mind that the prophets didn't tell us when the predicted events will happen and sometimes combine near and distant predictions in the same paragraph. . . . Sequence is a minor issue for the God who lives outside the constraints of time."

   What from this passage indicates that sequence was a minor issue for the prophet?

3. Sometimes the books of the prophets permit us to glimpse into the cosmic view of history—the history behind the history. In Daniel 10, for example, an angel explained to Daniel that "the prince of the Persian kingdom" had prevented him from answering Daniel's prayer for twenty-one days. Finally, reinforcements arrived, and Michael—a chief angel—helped him break through the opposition. So Daniel played a decisive role in the warfare between cosmic forces of good and evil, though much of the action was beyond his range of vision.

   Which portions of this passage are indicative of God's cosmic view—a view that we have a hard time grasping?

4. In what ways do you see God's personality—his thoughts, feelings, character—revealed through this passage?

5. Philip Yancey notes that "the prophets call us beyond the fears and grim reality of present history to the view of all eternity, to a time when God's reign will fill the earth with light and truth."

   Which portion(s) of this passage give you a glimpse of God's ultimate viewpoint and give you hope to endure the challenges of your life?

Perspective

The prophets . . . render God's point of view. God granted them (and, through them, us) the extraordinary vision to see past this world, dominated as it is by great powers and larger-than-life tyrants, to a different level of reality. We get a glimpse, a mere glimpse, of history from God's viewpoint. No wonder the prophets seem strange: we lack the capacity for seeing the world from the vantage point of timelessness.

—Philip Yancey

Group Discussion

1. Would one or two of you please share some highlights of your small group discussion with the whole group?

2. The following portion of ***The Bible Jesus Read*** captures beautifully the importance of the prophets' message for us today. Listen carefully:

   > In strange, complex images, the prophets present a wholly different view of the world. They offer hope, and something else: a challenge for us to live out the World as God Wants It in this life, right now. . . . What happens here on earth affects the future of the cosmos. From God's point of view, the future has already been determined, and the prophets spell out that future state in glowing detail: swords beaten into plowshares, a lamb recumbent beside a lion, a banquet feast. That is what God wants for this earth and that is what God will accomplish on this earth. The end is settled. What remains is whether we will live believing it.
   >
   > —Philip Yancey

   Why do you agree or disagree with this perspective? What difference might this perspective make to your life today?

> In strange, complex images, the prophets present a wholly different view of the world. They offer hope, and something else: a challenge for us to live out the World as God Wants It in this life, right now.... What happens here on earth affects the future of the cosmos. From God's point of view, the future has already been determined, and the prophets spell out that future state in glowing detail: swords beaten into plowshares, a lamb recumbent beside a lion, a banquet feast. That is what God wants for this earth and that is what God will accomplish on this earth. The end is settled. What remains is whether we will live believing it.
>
> —Philip Yancey

Why do you agree or disagree with this perspective? What difference might this perspective make to your life today?

Now it's time for each of us to consider on a personal level what we've been discussing and thinking about. Please turn to page 114.

5 min. PERSONAL JOURNEY: TO BEGIN NOW

Participant's Guide page 114.

Ironically, the seventeen most unread books of the Bible are the same books that give us the most complete picture of God's personality. With a passion that borders on the bizarre, the prophets proclaim to the human race that we matter to God. Over and over again, their urgent messages ring out to reveal a personal God who cares about every human being, who longs to be in relationship with us, and—above all—who loves us.

With this in mind, take some time now by yourself to consider the following questions.

1. Consider God's deep love for you—how he is always willing to forgive you, extend mercy to you, guide you. If he were to send a messenger—a prophet—to you as he did to the nations of Israel and Judah, what do you think he would say?
   a. How might he express his love in a way that is meaningful to you?
   b. What might he remind you he has done for you?
   c. How might he describe his greatest desires for your life or issue a word of warning?
2. In what way(s) can you express your thankfulness to him for his love and all that he has done for you?
3. In which area(s) of your life do you need to ask for his forgiveness so that your relationship with him can be all that he desires it to be?

NOTES

Group Discussion

1. **Would one or two of you please share some highlights of your small group discussion with the whole group?**

2. **The following portion of *The Bible Jesus Read* captures beautifully the importance of the prophets' message for us today. Listen carefully:**

> In strange, complex images, the prophets present a wholly different view of the world. They offer hope, and something else: a challenge for us to live out the World as God Wants It in this life, right now.... What happens here on earth affects the future of the cosmos. From God's point of view, the future has already been determined, and the prophets spell out that future state in glowing detail: swords beaten into plowshares, a lamb recumbent beside a lion, a banquet feast. That is what God wants for this earth and that is what God will accomplish on this earth. The end is settled. What remains is whether we will live believing it.
>
> —Philip Yancey

Why do you agree or disagree with this perspective? What difference might this perspective make to your life today?

Personal Journey: To Begin Now

Ironically, the seventeen most unread books of the Bible are the same books that give us the most complete picture of God's personality. With a passion that borders on the bizarre, the prophets proclaim to the human race that we matter to God. Over and over again, their urgent messages ring out to reveal a personal God who cares about every human being, who longs to be in relationship with us, and—above all—who loves us.

With this in mind, take some time now by yourself to consider the following questions.

1. Consider God's deep love for you—how he is always willing to forgive you, extend mercy to you, guide you. If he were to send a messenger—a prophet—to you as he did to the nations of Israel and Judah, what do you think he would say?

   a. How might God express his love in a way that is meaningful to you?

   b. What might God remind you he has done for you?

   c. How might God describe his greatest desires for your life or issue a word of warning?

2. **In what way(s) can you express your thankfulness to God for his love and all that he has done for you?**

3. **In which area(s) of your life do you need to ask for God's forgiveness so that your relationship with him can be all that he desires it to be?**

Let participants know when there is 1 minute remaining. Remind participants that they may want to continue their journey by completing the additional exercise on page 116 of their Participant's Guide before the next session.

PERSONAL JOURNEY: TO DO BETWEEN SESSIONS

The startling actions and mythic visions of the prophets seem strange to us because the prophets are revealing to mortal humans a glimpse of God's cosmic viewpoint. The prophets seek to open our eyes to the world as God sees it, and that viewpoint is, at best, difficult for us to grasp. Their messages transcend time, speaking to the present as well as to the future. If we will listen, we will gain a vision of what God is ultimately doing in the world and will receive hope to endure the challenges of the present.

With this in mind, before the next session, set aside time away from distractions to do the following exercise.

1. Make a list of the challenges you face in your life.
   a. Describe how these challenges appear from your viewpoint.
   b. From what you know of God and Scripture, how might God's viewpoint differ from yours?
   c. What thoughts and feelings arise as you consider God's viewpoint?
2. How we approach the challenges of life makes a big difference. Philip Yancey has discovered that the prophets have a very important message for us regarding our approach:

   > The prophets point us back to the present, yet ask us to live in the light of the future they image up. Can we trust their vision and accept it as the true reality of earth, despite all evidence to the contrary? Can we live now "as if" God is loving, gracious, merciful, and all-powerful? The prophets remind us that indeed God is and that history itself will one day bear that out. The World as It Is will become the World as God Wants It.

   Take another look at the challenges of your life and evaluate each one in terms of how it might be different if you lived "as if" God is loving, gracious, merciful, and all-powerful.

   a. In what way(s) might you change your approach to each challenge if you respond to it in light of the future God promises?
   b. Do you truly believe that God reigns even though this world shows little evidence of that? Why?

NOTES

Personal Journey: To Do between Sessions

The startling actions and mythic visions of the prophets seem strange to us because the prophets are revealing to mortal humans a glimpse of God's cosmic viewpoint. The prophets seek to open our eyes to the world as God sees it, and that viewpoint is, at best, difficult for us to grasp. Their messages transcend time, speaking to the present as well as to the future. If we will listen, we will gain a vision of what God is ultimately doing in the world and will receive hope to endure the challenges of the present.

1. Make a list of the challenges you face in your life.

   a. Describe how these challenges appear from your viewpoint.

   b. From what you know of God and Scripture, how might God's viewpoint differ from yours?

   c. What thoughts and feelings arise as you consider God's viewpoint?

2. How we approach the challenges of life makes a big difference. Philip Yancey has discovered that the prophets have a very important message for us regarding our approach:

   > The prophets point us back to the present, yet ask us to live in the light of the future they image up. Can we trust their vision and accept it as the true reality of earth, despite all evidence to the contrary? Can we live now "as if" God is loving, gracious, merciful, and all-powerful? The prophets remind us that indeed God is and that history itself will one day bear that out. The World as It Is will become the World as God Wants It.

   Take another look at the challenges of your life and evaluate each one in terms of how it might be different if you lived "as if" God is loving, gracious, merciful, and all-powerful.

   a. In what way(s) might you change your approach to each challenge if you respond to it in light of the future God promises?

   b. Do you truly believe that God reigns even though this world shows little evidence of that? Why?

c. Do you trust God enough to be able to rest in his powerful, loving embrace even though you live in dangerous, chaotic times? Explain what difference this will make in how you live.

d. Evaluate your desire to know God on an intimate, personal level and to take on his heart and passion.

Changing our perspective and approach is quite an adventure in faith. These questions cannot be answered easily and put aside. They should remain before us daily as we seek to know God and grow in our relationship with him.

Perspective

If only we could believe that our struggle really is against principalities and powers, if only we could believe that God will prove himself trustworthy and set right all that is wrong, if only we could demonstrate God's passion for justice and truth in this world—then, I think, the prophets will have accomplished their most urgent mission.

—Philip Yancey

1 min. CLOSING MEDITATION

Let's take a moment to close in prayer.

Dear God, we praise your name. You are great and most worthy of praise. For generations people have shared stories of all the things you have done and told of your goodness and awesome works. You have such deep love and compassion for each of us, and you are faithful to keep all your promises to us. We look to you to meet our deepest needs. You are near each of us who calls to you. Thank you for revealing so much of yourself in the books of the prophets. Draw us closer to you. In Jesus' most precious name we pray, amen.

–Prayer inspired by Psalm 145

NOTES

c. Do you trust God enough to be able to rest in his powerful, loving embrace even though you live in dangerous, chaotic times? Explain what difference this will make in how you live.

d. Evaluate your desire to know God on an intimate, personal level and to take on his heart and passion.

Changing our perspective and approach is quite an adventure in faith. These questions cannot be answered easily and put aside. They should remain before us daily as we seek to know God and grow in our relationship with him.

Perspective

If only we could believe that our struggle really is against principalities and powers, if only we could believe that God will prove himself trustworthy and set right all that is wrong, if only we could demonstrate God's passion for justice and truth in this world—then, I think, the prophets will have accomplished their most urgent mission.

—Philip Yancey

SESSION EIGHT

Advance Echoes of a Final Answer

BEFORE YOU LEAD

Synopsis

This final session, which serves as a wrap-up for the series, brings the Old and New Testaments together, showing how the coming of the Messiah is the culmination of the Hebrews' story. "In a sense," Philip Yancey writes, "all of Old Testament history serves as a preparation for Jesus, with the characters on its pages contributing a family, an identity, and a race for Jesus to be born into. What did God have in mind with the long, convoluted story of the Hebrews? The answer of the New Testament is unequivocal: Jesus is what God had in mind. He came to reconcile humanity to God by extending God's kingdom beyond the boundaries of race to the entire world."

The Old and New Testaments complement each other, and each is fundamentally incomplete without the other. When Jesus came to earth, he linked himself strongly to the Old Testament. It was, of course, the only Bible he knew, the Scriptures he listened to, read, and studied from his earliest years. Throughout his ministry on earth, Jesus pointed out repeatedly that he was the fulfillment of all that had been written before in the Scriptures. The New Testament writers emphasized this unity as well. In fact, much of the New Testament makes sense only when we understand the history of God's chosen family as recorded in the Old Testament.

Much of the Old Testament records a longing for Messiah, the one who satisfies our human longings for hope, meaning, strength, peace, and faith. These longings are not unique to the Old Testament writers; they reflect the longings of every human heart. Thus the Old Testament writings, laced with honest realism and passionate emotion, touch a deep chord within us. The questions, fears, and doubts they boldly voice echo in our own souls. As we read the words of those who have gone before us, we find comfort, reassurance, and hope for the struggles we face.

The key questions the Old Testament writers raised are fundamental to human existence–"Do I matter?" "Does God care?" "Why doesn't God act?" The Old Testament writers believed that these anguished questions would find at least partial resolution in the coming of the Messiah, and the New Testament affirms that Jesus answers them. We'll also note how insignificant these questions seemed to be to the New Testament writers. Perhaps they didn't focus on these questions because Jesus was with them and they saw the answers revealed through his physical presence every day.

As he concludes his video comments, Philip Yancey suggests that we take various psalms–prayers written to God–and make them our prayers by substituting the details of our lives for the details the psalmists described. He also reminds us of God's timeless perspective and his faithfulness in accomplishing all that he wants to accomplish–not necessarily in the way we would expect, but in his perfect time.

Key Points of This Session

1. The Old and New Testaments complement each other, and are, in fact, incomplete without the other. Jesus is the completion, the fulfillment, of the Old Testament promises. The Old Testament is essential to understanding Jesus and the New Testament.
2. The Old Testament expresses our deepest longings and the questions that haunt our hearts. Although they at times were plagued by doubt and disappointment, the Old Testament writers still focus our eyes on the hope of the promises God has made in response to our longings. The realism and honesty of these writers as they waited for God to act provides comfort and encouragement to us as we, too, await the final unfolding of God's promises.

Suggested Reading

This session corresponds to Chapter 7 of *The Bible Jesus Read.* You may want to read this chapter in order to deepen your understanding of this material.

Session Outline (52 minutes)

- I. Introduction (5 minutes)
  - A. Welcome
  - B. What's to Come
  - C. Questions to Think About
- II. Video Presentation: "Advance Echoes of a Final Answer" (11 minutes)
- III. Group Discovery (30 minutes)
  - A. Video Highlights (5 minutes)
  - B. Large Group Exploration: The Messiah—God's Answer to the Longings of His People (10 minutes)
  - C. Small Group Exploration: Do We Matter to God? (10 minutes)
  - D. Group Discussion (5 minutes)
- IV. Personal Journey (5 minutes)
- V. Closing Meditation (1 minute)

Materials

You'll need a VCR, TV, and Bible. You may also find a whiteboard, flip chart, or overhead projector to be a useful tool in guiding group discussion. View the video prior to leading the session so you are familiar with its main points.

SESSION EIGHT

Advance Echoes of a Final Answer

In a sense, all of Old Testament history serves as a preparation for Jesus, with the characters on its pages contributing a family, an identity, and a race for Jesus to be born into. What did God have in mind with the long, convoluted story of the Hebrews? The answer of the New Testament is unequivocal: Jesus is what God had in mind. He came to reconcile humanity to God by extending God's kingdom beyond the boundaries of race to the entire world.

—Philip Yancey

5 min. INTRODUCTION

Welcome

Welcome participants to Session 8 of *The Bible Jesus Read* course: "Advance Echoes of a Final Answer."

What's to Come

In this session we'll see how the Old and New Testaments complement each other and how the Old Testament anticipates the coming of the Messiah. We'll consider how Jesus answered some of the deepest longings and most nagging questions raised by the Old Testament prophets: "Do we matter to God?" "Does God care?" "Why doesn't God act?" We will also consider the questions, fears, and doubts the Old Testament writers boldly voiced that echo in our own souls. In their words we will find comfort, reassurance, and hope for facing our struggles.

Let's begin by considering a few questions. Please turn to page 119 of your Participant's Guide.

Questions to Think About

Participants Guide page 119.

As time permits, ask two or more of the following questions and solicit responses from the participants.

NOTES

SESSION EIGHT

Advance Echoes of a Final Answer

In a sense, all of Old Testament history serves as a preparation for Jesus, with the characters on its pages contributing a family, an identity, and a race for Jesus to be born into. What did God have in mind with the long, convoluted story of the Hebrews? The answer of the New Testament is unequivocal: Jesus is what God had in mind. He came to reconcile humanity to God by extending God's kingdom beyond the boundaries of race to the entire world.

—Philip Yancey

Questions to Think About

1. If someone were to ask you, "What does the Old Testament offer to Christians today?" or "Why should a Christian read the Old Testament?" what would you say?

1. If someone were to ask you, "What does the Old Testament offer to Christians today?" or "Why should a Christian read the Old Testament?" what would you say?

Responses will vary and may include such benefits as providing an intimate picture of a personal God, a realistic view of our human tendency to ignore God, encouragement to be really honest with God, etc. By this point, participants should have gained an appreciation of the Old Testament and be able to identify its value to them. This session should add to that appreciation and value.

2. In what way(s) has the Old Testament story and the way the Old Testament writers present it deepened your walk with God? Compare the benefits the Old Testament brings to your spiritual life with the contributions of the New Testament.

The intent here is to encourage participants to begin thinking of the relationship and impact of both the Old and New Testaments on God's redemptive plan for the world and on their daily spiritual life.

3. How would you describe the personality of God revealed in the Old Testament as compared to the New Testament? In what way(s) has your perception changed as a result of our study?

A typical stereotype is that the God of the Old Testament is a stern judge while the God of the New Testament is a merciful, nice person. Most participants will now realize that this stereotype does not hold up. The God of the Old Testament is incredibly loving and merciful, caring and compassionate. He also hates sin and punishes disobedience. Jesus, in the New Testament, demonstrates love and mercy but also speaks of judgment to come.

Let's keep these ideas in mind as we view the video. There is space to take notes on page 121.

11 min. VIDEO PRESENTATION: "ADVANCE ECHOES OF A FINAL ANSWER"

Participant's Guide page 121.

Leader's Video Observations

The Old and New Testaments: both are necessary

NOTES

SESSION EIGHT

Advance Echoes of a Final Answer

In a sense, all of Old Testament history serves as a preparation for Jesus, with the characters on its pages contributing a family, an identity, and a race for Jesus to be born into. What did God have in mind with the long, convoluted story of the Hebrews? The answer of the New Testament is unequivocal: Jesus is what God had in mind. He came to reconcile humanity to God by extending God's kingdom beyond the boundaries of race to the entire world.

—Philip Yancey

Questions to Think About

1. If someone were to ask you, "What does the Old Testament offer to Christians today?" or "Why should a Christian read the Old Testament?" what would you say?

2. In what way(s) has the Old Testament story and the way the Old Testament writers present it deepened your walk with God? Compare the benefits the Old Testament brings to your spiritual life with the contributions of the New Testament.

3. How would you describe the personality of God revealed in the Old Testament as compared to the New Testament? In what way(s) has your perception changed as a result of our study?

Video Presentation: "Advance Echoes of a Final Answer"

The Old and New Testaments: both are necessary

The Old Testament story: a longing for Jesus

Finding comfort in the Old Testament

Making the Old Testament our own

A testimony to God's timeless work

The Old Testament story: a longing for Jesus

Finding comfort in the Old Testament

Making the Old Testament our own

A testimony to God's timeless work

30 min. GROUP DISCOVERY

If your group has seven or more members, use the Video Highlights with the entire group (5 minutes), then complete the Large Group Exploration (10 minutes), and then break into small groups of three to five people for the Small Group Exploration (10 minutes). Finally, bring everyone together for the closing Group Discussion (5 minutes).

If your group has fewer than seven members, begin with the Video Highlights (5 minutes), then complete both the Large Group Exploration (10 minutes) and the Small Group Exploration (10 minutes) as a group. Wrap up your discovery time with the Group Discussion (5 minutes).

Please turn to page 122 as we discuss some questions related to the video segment we have just seen.

Video Highlights (5 minutes)

Participant's Guide page 122.

As time permits, ask one or more of the following questions, which directly relate to the video the participants have just seen.

NOTES

Video Presentation: "Advance Echoes of a Final Answer"

The Old and New Testaments: both are necessary

The Old Testament story: a longing for Jesus

Finding comfort in the Old Testament

Making the Old Testament our own

A testimony to God's timeless work

1. In what ways do you see the Old and New Testaments complementing and completing one another?

The intent here is to explore participants' understanding of this concept and to encourage them to look for the unity of the Old and New Testaments, not to convince them of a particular viewpoint. Some will agree that the Old Testament sets the stage for the New Testament. Jewish people will disagree, since their Bible consists only of the Old Testament. Some will understand the Old Testament more clearly once the New Testament perspective is superimposed on it. Some participants may not have enough experience with the Bible to really see the continuity of Old and New Testaments.

2. Philip Yancey believes we "truly understand Jesus only by reading the Old Testament." In what way(s) do you see the Old Testament contributing to our understanding of Jesus?

Jesus often referred to Old Testament images and symbols in his teaching, so our understanding of his teaching is limited without the background of the Old Testament. When we become more familiar with the Old Testament, we are becoming more familiar with the Scriptures Jesus read, memorized, and taught. We also learn the story of the Hebrews, as we saw in Session 2, and that story gives us a context for understanding the promised Messiah—and Jesus' eventual birth, death, and resurrection.

3. This video portrays the Old Testament as having very personal overtones–being a source of comfort, an expression of the universal longings of the human heart. This perspective differs from a view of the Old Testament as being merely the history of the Hebrews and the source of the Ten Commandments. How have you traditionally viewed the Old Testament, and what are your responses to the perspective presented in this video?

There are no "right" or "wrong" answers here. Allow participants to share their developing understanding and appreciation of the Old Testament. Some participants may have difficulty adjusting to this perspective, while others will connect with it right away. Allow them to share their surprises, questions, and even conflicts.

Now we're ready for the Large Group Exploration part of this session. Please turn to page 123.

Large Group Exploration: The Messiah–God's Answer to the Longings of His People (10 minutes)

Participant's Guide page 123.

Read the introductory paragraphs to the group, then begin discussing the Scripture texts that follow.

NOTES

Video Highlights

1. In what ways do you see the Old and New Testaments complementing and completing one another?

2. Philip Yancey believes we "truly understand Jesus only by reading the Old Testament." In what way(s) do you see the Old Testament contributing to our understanding of Jesus?

3. This video portrays the Old Testament as having very personal overtones—being a source of comfort, an expression of the universal longings of the human heart. This perspective differs from a view of the Old Testament as being merely the history of the Hebrews and the source of the Ten Commandments. How have you traditionally viewed the Old Testament, and what are your responses to the perspective presented in this video?

As he considers the Old Testament writings, Philip Yancey sees its writers expressing deep longings that are common to every human heart. These longings can be expressed in terms of three broad questions. He writes, "I return again and again to the Old Testament because it faces head-on these very questions. 'Do I matter?' 'Does God care?' 'Why doesn't God act?'"

The Old Testament writers, particularly the psalmists and prophets, eagerly pointed to a time when God would address these deep longings and answer the unanswered questions. They envisioned at least partial resolution to these longings at the coming of the Messiah. Let's consider some of these longings as they are brought to fruition in the person of Jesus.

1. Isaiah 42–53 records specific promises God gave in response to these longings and questions. First, let's look at some of the promises God made that boldly foretold the Incarnation—God's ultimate answer. Then, let's consider how the New Testament affirms that Jesus fulfilled God's promises.

Longings and Questions	**What God Promised to Do**	**New Testament Affirmations that Jesus Fulfilled these Promises**
Longing for justice	Isaiah 42:1–4: To send his chosen one who would bring justice to the nations and establish justice on earth.	Matthew 12:15–21; Acts 17:29–31: Jesus knew that he fulfilled the Isaiah 42:1–4 prophecy, and Paul referred to Jesus, who would judge the world with justice.
Longing for God's presence with his people	Isaiah 42:5–7: The one he sent would be a covenant for the people, a light for the Gentiles, and would open blind eyes and free captives imprisoned in sin.	Matthew 26:28; Luke 2:25–32: Jesus' blood of the covenant brought forgiveness of sins; Simeon realized Jesus would bring the Gentiles light.
Longing for God to act	Isaiah 43:19: To do something new.	Mark 1:27; 2 Corinthians 5:17–19: People recognized Jesus' new teaching; new believers are a new, redeemed creation of God.
Longing for forgiveness and redemption	Isaiah 43:25; 44:21–23: To forgive all their sins and remember them no more; redeem his people.	Matthew 26:27–28; Romans 8:1–4; 1 John 1:9: Jesus forgave people's sins; Jesus' blood brought forgiveness of sin.

NOTES

Large Group Exploration: The Messiah—God's Answer to the Longings of His People

As he considers the Old Testament writings, Philip Yancey sees its writers expressing deep longings common to every human heart. These longings can be expressed in terms of three broad questions. He writes, "I return again and again to the Old Testament because it faces head-on these very questions. 'Do I matter?' 'Does God care?' 'Why doesn't God act?'"

The Old Testament writers, particularly the psalmists and prophets, eagerly pointed to a time when God would address these deep longings and answer the unanswered questions. They envisioned at least partial resolution to these longings at the coming of the Messiah. Let's consider some of these longings as they are brought to fruition in the person of Jesus.

1. Isaiah 42–53 records specific promises God gave in response to these longings and questions. First, let's look at some of the promises God made that boldly foretold the Incarnation–God's ultimate answer. Then, let's consider how the New Testament affirms that Jesus fulfilled God's promises.

Longings and Questions	What God Promised to Do	New Testament Affirmations that Jesus Fulfilled these Promises
Longing for justice	Isaiah 42:1–4:	Matthew 12:15–21; Acts 17:29–31:
Longing for God's presence with his people	Isaiah 42: 5–7:	Matthew 26:28; Luke 2:25–32:
Longing for God to act	Isaiah 43:19:	Mark 1:27; 2 Corinthians 5:17–19:
Longing for forgiveness and redemption	Isaiah 43:25; 44:21–23:	Matthew 26:27–28; Romans 8:1–4; 1 John 1:9:
Has God forsaken us?	Isaiah 49:14–16:	John 3:16; Romans 8:38; Hebrews 13:5:
Why do the wicked prosper?	Isaiah 51:4–8:	Matthew 13:40–43; 25:41–46; 2 Peter 3:10–13:

2. "Whenever I read straight through the Bible," Philip Yancey writes, "a huge difference between the Old and New Testaments comes to light. In the Old Testament I can find many expressions of doubt and disappointment.... In striking contrast, the New Testament Epistles contain little of this type of anguish. The problem of pain surely has not gone away ... Nevertheless, nowhere do I find the piercing question, Does God care? ... The reason for the change, I believe, is that Jesus answered that question for the witnesses who wrote the Epistles."

   Read Romans 5:1–8. In what way(s) do you recognize the difference Philip Yancey noted between the Old Testament perspective and the New Testament perspective?

Longings and Questions	What God Promised to Do	New Testament Affirmations that Jesus Fulfilled these Promises
Has God forsaken us?	Isaiah 49:14–16: Not forget his people, using the illustration of a mother who can't forget a baby she is nursing. God said he had engraved them on the palms of his hands.	John 3:16; Romans 8:38; Hebrews 13:5: God loves people so much that he sent Jesus to die for us so our sins can be forgiven; absolutely nothing can separate us from God's love; God has promised not to forsake us.
Why do the wicked prosper?	Isaiah 51:4–8: Send justice and that righteous people who obey God will triumph in the end. The heavens will vanish, but his salvation and righteousness will last forever.	Matthew 13:40–43; 25:41–46; 2 Peter 3:10–13: One day everyone will be judged; heaven and earth will pass away; righteous people will receive eternal life, the unrighteous will receive eternal punishment; there will be a new heaven and earth.

2. "Whenever I read straight through the Bible," Philip Yancey writes, "a huge difference between the Old and New Testaments comes to light. In the Old Testament I can find many expressions of doubt and disappointment.... In striking contrast, the New Testament Epistles contain little of this type of anguish. The problem of pain surely has not gone away ... Nevertheless, nowhere do I find the piercing question, *Does God care?* ... The reason for the change, I believe, is that Jesus answered that question for the witnesses who wrote the Epistles."

   Read Romans 5:1–8. In what way(s) do you recognize the difference Philip Yancey noted between the Old Testament perspective and the New Testament perspective?

The difference is so striking, it is exciting! This passage presents a whole different tone—one of hope and rejoicing in the face of suffering. The writer clearly attributed his upbeat tone to the presence of Jesus—the Messiah who came just as God promised.

Please turn to page 126 as we move into the Small Group Exploration part of this session.

NOTES

Longing for forgiveness and redemption	Isaiah 43:25; 44:21–23:	Matthew 26:27–28; Romans 8:1–4; 1 John 1:9:
Has God forsaken us?	Isaiah 49:14–16:	John 3:16; Romans 8:38; Hebrews 13:5:
Why do the wicked prosper?	Isaiah 51:4–8:	Matthew 13:40–43; 25:41–46; 2 Peter 3:10–13:

2. "Whenever I read straight through the Bible," Philip Yancey writes, "a huge difference between the Old and New Testaments comes to light. In the Old Testament I can find many expressions of doubt and disappointment.... In striking contrast, the New Testament Epistles contain little of this type of anguish. The problem of pain surely has not gone away ... Nevertheless, nowhere do I find the piercing question, Does God care? ... The reason for the change, I believe, is that Jesus answered that question for the witnesses who wrote the Epistles."

   Read Romans 5:1–8. In what way(s) do you recognize the difference Philip Yancey noted between the Old Testament perspective and the New Testament perspective?

Perspective

I have learned to love the Old Testament because it so poignantly expresses my own inner longings. I find in it a realism about human nature that is sorely absent from much smiley-face Christian propaganda. And yet the Old Testament writers, especially the psalmists and prophets, eagerly point ahead to a time when God has vowed to address those longings, to answer the questions that never go away.

—Philip Yancey

Small Group Exploration: Do We Matter to God? (10 minutes)

Participant's Guide page 126.

Years ago the psalmist asked, "What is man that you are mindful of him?" (Psalm 8:4). Although we may word it differently, that question still echoes in the human heart. Each of us wants to know if we really matter to God, if God truly loves and cares for us as individuals. The coming of the Messiah, the birth of Jesus on this earth, answered that question with a resounding "yes!"

"In effect," Philip Yancey writes, "the holiday we celebrate as Christmas memorializes God's answer to the Hebrews' question, *Do we matter?* Here on earth, for thirty-three years, God experienced in flesh what it is like to be one of us. In the stories he told, and the people whose lives he touched, Jesus answered for all time that vexing question."

After breaking into groups of three to five, have someone in your group read the Scripture passage listed.

If you will not be breaking into small groups for the Small Group Exploration, lead the group in a discussion of the following questions.

1. One way Jesus communicated God's love for us was through the parables he told. Read the following parables. In each case, how did Jesus show we matter to God?

   a. Luke 15:1–7

Just as a competent, loving shepherd will leave ninety-nine sheep to find one that is lost, God cares about every person. When a sinner repents, all heaven rejoices! This shows just how much God loves each of us and how much he desires a personal relationship with us.

   b. Luke 15:11–24

In this parable, the father of the wayward son couldn't stop thinking about him. In fact, his father saw him when he "was still a long way off." Likewise, God is always longing for us and is ready to receive us when we come to him.

NOTES

Perspective

I have learned to love the Old Testament because it so poignantly expresses my own inner longings. I find in it a realism about human nature that is sorely absent from much smiley-face Christian propaganda. And yet the Old Testament writers, especially the psalmists and prophets, eagerly point ahead to a time when God has vowed to address those longings, to answer the questions that never go away.
—Philip Yancey

Small Group Exploration: Do We Matter to God?

Years ago the psalmist asked, "What is man that you are mindful of him?" (Psalm 8:4). Although we may word it differently, that question still echoes in the human heart. Each of us wants to know if we really matter to God, if God truly loves and cares for us as individuals. The coming of the Messiah, the birth of Jesus on this earth, answered that question with a resounding "yes!"

"In effect," Philip Yancey writes, "the holiday we celebrate as Christmas memorializes God's answer to the Hebrews' question, *Do we matter?* Here on earth, for thirty-three years, God experienced in flesh what it is like to be one of us. In the stories he told, and the people whose lives he touched, Jesus answered for all time that vexing question."

After breaking into groups of three to five, have someone in your group read the Scripture passage listed.

1. One way Jesus communicated God's love for us was through the parables he told. Read the following parables. In each case, how did Jesus show we matter to God?

   a. Luke 15:1–7

   b. Luke 15:11–24

2. It isn't enough to be told we matter; we long to see proof in action. Repeatedly, Jesus showed people who didn't matter to society that they mattered to God. What outstanding demonstration of this do we see in Matthew 8:1–3?

2. It isn't enough to be told we matter; we long to see proof in action. Repeatedly, Jesus showed people who didn't matter to society that they mattered to God. What outstanding demonstration of this do we see in Matthew 8:1–3?

Jesus touched a person with leprosy—an outcast among outcasts—and healed him. No one in Jesus' day would touch a leprosy victim.

3. To show how very much we matter to him, what ultimate sacrifice did Jesus make for each of us? (See John 3:16; 1 John 4:10.)

God sent Jesus—the promised Messiah—to earth to be sacrificed for our sins. Through Jesus, we can receive forgiveness of sins and eternal life.

4. When we are suffering or are in pain, it's easy to wonder if God still cares. Two instances in the Gospels especially show the compassionate, caring heart of God. How did Jesus respond in each instance?

   a. John 11:1–3, 17–19, 32–36

After Lazarus died, Jesus went to Bethany to comfort the sisters of Lazarus. There, because of his love, Jesus wept.

   b. Luke 19:41–44

Jesus wept when he looked out over Jerusalem and realized what would happen to the city and his people in the future. The suffering they would endure overwhelmed him with grief.

Did You Know?

We *matter* to God. In a rare moment when he pulled back the curtain between seen and unseen worlds, Jesus said that angels rejoice when a single sinner repents. A solitary act on this speck of a planet reverberates throughout the cosmos.

—Philip Yancey

If you have divided into small groups, let participants know when there is 1 minute remaining.

Give participants a moment to transition from their small group discussions. If time allows, or if you have assigned each group a specific question, have representatives from the groups share their key ideas.

Now let's wrap up our Group Discovery time. Please turn to page 128.

NOTES

Small Group Exploration: Do We Matter to God?

Years ago the psalmist asked, "What is man that you are mindful of him?" (Psalm 8:4). Although we may word it differently, that question still echoes in the human heart. Each of us wants to know if we really matter to God, if God truly loves and cares for us as individuals. The coming of the Messiah, the birth of Jesus on this earth, answered that question with a resounding "yes!"

"In effect," Philip Yancey writes, "the holiday we celebrate as Christmas memorializes God's answer to the Hebrews' question, *Do we matter?* Here on earth, for thirty-three years, God experienced in flesh what it is like to be one of us. In the stories he told, and the people whose lives he touched, Jesus answered for all time that vexing question."

After breaking into groups of three to five, have someone in your group read the Scripture passage listed.

1. One way Jesus communicated God's love for us was through the parables he told. Read the following parables. In each case, how did Jesus show we matter to God?

   a. Luke 15:1–7

   b. Luke 15:11–24

2. It isn't enough to be told we matter; we long to see proof in action. Repeatedly, Jesus showed people who didn't matter to society that they mattered to God. What outstanding demonstration of this do we see in Matthew 8:1–3?

3. To show how very much we matter to him, what ultimate sacrifice did Jesus make for each of us? (See John 3:16; 1 John 4:10.)

4. When we are suffering or are in pain, it's easy to wonder if God still cares. Two instances in the Gospels especially show the compassionate, caring heart of God. How did Jesus respond in each instance?

   a. John 11:1–3, 17–19, 32–36

   b. Luke 19:41–44

Did You Know?

We *matter* to God. In a rare moment when he pulled back the curtain between seen and unseen worlds, Jesus said that angels rejoice when a single sinner repents. A solitary act on this speck of a planet reverberates throughout the cosmos.

—Philip Yancey

Group Discussion (5 minutes)

Participant's Guide page 128.

Use one or more of the following questions to encourage participants to share their observations with the entire group.

1. The realism of the Old Testament—people's doubts, questions, struggles—first attracted Philip Yancey and then captured his attention. In what way(s) has God been changing your views of the Old Testament since we started this series? What has drawn you to value more highly the Old Testament?
2. After the Old Testament writings were completed, God was silent for four hundred years. Then he finally *acted* by sending the Messiah. In what ways does the coming of the Messiah affirm to you that you matter, that God cares, and that God does take action (albeit on his own timetable)?
3. Philip Yancey has come to believe that when we add Jesus to the Old Testament story, things fall into place differently than if we read the Old Testament without him. In what way(s) do you agree or disagree?
4. What excites you most about the opportunity to read and study more of the Old Testament as a result of what you have learned during this group study?

Perspective

To the question, *Why doesn't God act?* Jews and Christians have the same answer, with one crucial difference. Jews believe that God will act, by sending the Messiah. Christians believe that God has acted, by sending the Messiah, and will act once more, by sending him again, this time in power and glory, not in weakness and humility.

—Philip Yancey

Now it's time for each of us to consider on a personal level what we've been discussing and thinking about. Please turn to page 130.

5 min. PERSONAL JOURNEY: TO BEGIN NOW

Participant's Guide page 130.

The Old and New Testaments complement each other, and are, in fact, incomplete without the other. Jesus is the completion, the fulfillment, of the Old Testament promises. The Old Testament is essential to understanding Jesus and the New Testament.

NOTES

Group Discussion

1. The realism of the Old Testament—people's doubts, questions, struggles—first attracted Philip Yancey and then captured his attention. In what way(s) has God been changing your views of the Old Testament since we started this series? What has drawn you to value more highly the Old Testament?

2. After the Old Testament writings were completed, God was silent for four hundred years. Then he finally *acted* by sending the Messiah. In what ways does the coming of the Messiah affirm to you that you matter, that God cares, and that God does take action (albeit on his own timetable)?

3. Philip Yancey has come to believe that when we add Jesus to the Old Testament story, things fall into place differently than if we read the Old Testament without him. In what way(s) do you agree or disagree?

4. What excites you most about the opportunity to read and study more of the Old Testament as a result of what you have learned during this group study?

Perspective

To the question, *Why doesn't God act?* Jews and Christians have the same answer, with one crucial difference. Jews believe that God will act, by sending the Messiah. Christians believe that God has acted, by sending the Messiah, and will act once more, by sending him again, this time in power and glory, not in weakness and humility.

—Philip Yancey

Personal Journey: To Begin Now

The Old and New Testaments complement each other, and are, in fact, incomplete without the other. Jesus is the completion, the fulfillment, of the Old Testament promises. The Old Testament is essential to understanding Jesus and the New Testament.

With this in mind, take some time now by yourself to respond to the following questions.

1. Continuing to become more familiar with the Old Testament can open up whole new areas to us in our spiritual walk.

   a. What would be the benefits to you of continuing to search out and grow in your knowledge and understanding of the Old Testament?

   b. Describe some ways in which you will continue exploring the Old Testament during the days and weeks ahead. (These might include following a reading plan, using a concordance and/or study Bible to trace specific references Jesus made to the Old Testament, using a study Bible or other reference to better understand the Old Testament images Jesus used in his teachings, etc.)

With this in mind, take some time now by yourself to consider the following questions.

1. Continuing to become more familiar with the Old Testament can open up whole new areas to us in our spiritual walk.
   a. What would be the benefits to you of continuing to search out and grow in your knowledge and understanding of the Old Testament?
   b. Describe some ways in which you will continue exploring the Old Testament during the days and weeks ahead. (These might include following a reading plan, using a concordance and/or study Bible to trace specific references Jesus made to the Old Testament, using a study Bible or other reference to better understand the Old Testament images Jesus used in his teachings, etc.)
   c. What is your commitment to begin reading the Old Testament regularly?
2. Write down the Bible passages that mean a great deal to you. Are most of them from the Old Testament or New Testament? Why do you think you have chosen these passages?

Let participants know when there is 1 minute remaining. Remind participants that they may want to continue their journey by completing the additional exercise on page 132 of their Participant's Guide before the next session.

PERSONAL JOURNEY

The Old Testament expresses our deepest longings and the questions that haunt our hearts. Although they at times were plagued by doubt and disappointment, the Old Testament writers still focus our eyes on the hope of the promises God has made in response to our longings. The realism and honesty of these writers as they waited for God to act provides comfort and encouragement to us as we, too, await the final unfolding of God's promises.

With that in mind, set aside time away from distractions to do the following exercise.

1. In which area(s) of your life right now do you need comfort? Make a list of any struggles, doubts, longings, discouragements, fears, and pain you are having a hard time coping with on your own.
   a. In what way(s) does the message that you matter to God, that he cares for you, and that he has (and will) take action impact your personal struggles and longings?

NOTES

Personal Journey: To Begin Now

The Old and New Testaments complement each other, and are, in fact, incomplete without the other. Jesus is the completion, the fulfillment, of the Old Testament promises. The Old Testament is essential to understanding Jesus and the New Testament.

With this in mind, take some time now by yourself to respond to the following questions.

1. Continuing to become more familiar with the Old Testament can open up whole new areas to us in our spiritual walk.
   a. What would be the benefits to you of continuing to search out and grow in your knowledge and understanding of the Old Testament?
   b. Describe some ways in which you will continue exploring the Old Testament during the days and weeks ahead. (These might include following a reading plan, using a concordance and/or study Bible to trace specific references Jesus made to the Old Testament, using a study Bible or other reference to better understand the Old Testament images Jesus used in his teachings, etc.)

   c. What is your commitment to begin reading the Old Testament regularly?

2. Write down the Bible passages that mean a great deal to you. Are most of them from the Old Testament or New Testament? Why do you think you have chosen these passages?

Personal Journey

The Old Testament expresses our deepest longings and the questions that haunt our hearts. Although they at times were plagued by doubt and disappointment, the Old Testament writers still focus our eyes on the hope of the promises God has made in response to our longings. The realism and honesty of these writers as they waited for God to act provides comfort and encouragement to us as we, too, await the final unfolding of God's promises.

1. In which area(s) of your life right now do you need comfort? Make a list of any struggles, doubts, longings, discouragements, fears, and pain you are having a hard time coping with on your own.
   a. In what way(s) does the message that you matter to God, that he cares for you, and that he has (and will) take action impact your personal struggles and longings?

b. What do you expect Jesus to do to meet you in your struggles and longings? How have you expressed those feelings to God?

2. Sometimes it is difficult for us to express our deepest feelings and needs to God. We may be too afraid or too weary to do so, but God still wants us to share our hearts with him. The Old Testament writers held nothing back when they opened their hearts to God. Sometimes, when we are incapable of expressing ourselves to God, *their* words express our thoughts exactly. Spend some time browsing the psalms. When you find a psalm that touches your heart, substitute details from your life into the psalm, and make it your own prayer to God.

Perspective

My father-in-law, Hunter Norwood, lived a rich, full life of eighty years. He sailed to South America as a missionary in 1942, built a house in the jungle by hand, founded a church and Bible Institute, and later returned to the U.S. to direct a mission organization. He was known by many as a Bible teacher *par excellence*. Eventually, due to cancer and a nerve-degenerating disease, he could no longer teach the Bible, but he continued to study it faithfully each day.

As his illness progressed, Hunter's world shrank to the size of a hospital bed, which he rarely left. Those of us who knew him well know that the last few years of his life were by far the hardest. Opponents of his faith had stoned him in Columbia. He had coped with alligators, boa constrictors, and piranhas in Peru. He had raised six daughters in two different cultures. But none of these compared to the difficulties of lying in bed all day, his body defying his every command, waiting to die. Toward the end, it took all his effort to accomplish the simple acts of swallowing and breathing.

It is hard to maintain a spirit of joy and victory when your body rebels against you, when you must call for help to drink a glass of water or blow your nose. As we are inclined to do, Hunter went through a crisis of faith during those last few years, but he never stopped relating to God. Until the day he could no longer hold a pen, he recorded a journal of his wrestling with God. As I studied the hundreds of entries in that journal, I found only nine entries referring to New Testament texts. All the others are from the Old Testament.

The wavering yet rock-solid faith Hunter found in the Old Testament sustained him when nothing else could. Even at his most doubt-filled moments, he took comfort in the fact that some of God's favorites had battled the very same demons. He learned that the arms of the Lord are long and wrap around those he loves. I am glad that, in those dark days, Hunter Norwood had the Old Testament to fall back on.

—Philip Yancey

NOTES

b. What do you expect Jesus to do to meet you in your struggles and longings? How have you expressed those feelings to God?

2. Sometimes it is difficult for us to express our deepest feelings and needs to God. We may be too afraid or too weary to do so, but God still wants us to share our hearts with him. The Old Testament writers held nothing back when they opened their hearts to God. Sometimes, when we are incapable of expressing ourselves to God, *their* words express our thoughts exactly. Spend some time browsing the psalms. When you find a psalm that touches your heart, substitute details from your life into the psalm, and make it your own prayer to God.

Perspective

My father-in-law, Hunter Norwood, lived a rich, full life of eighty years. He sailed to South America as a missionary in 1942, built a house in the jungle by hand, founded a church and Bible Institute, and later returned to the U.S. to direct a mission organization. He was known by many as a Bible teacher *par excellence*. Eventually, due to cancer and a nerve-degenerating disease, he could no longer teach the Bible, but he continued to study it faithfully each day.

As his illness progressed, Hunter's world shrank to the size of a hospital bed, which he rarely left. Those of us who knew him well know that the last few years of his life were by far the hardest. Opponents of his faith had stoned him in Columbia. He had coped with alligators, boa constrictors, and piranhas in Peru. He had raised six daughters in two different cultures. But none of these compared to the difficulties of lying in bed all day, his body defying his every command, waiting to die. Toward the end, it took all his effort to accomplish the simple acts of swallowing and breathing.

It is hard to maintain a spirit of joy and victory when your body rebels against you, when you must call for help to drink a glass of water or blow your nose. As we are inclined to do, Hunter went through a crisis of faith during those last few years, but he never stopped relating to God. Until the day he could no longer hold a pen, he recorded a journal of his wrestling with God. As I studied the hundreds of entries in that journal, I found only nine entries referring to New Testament texts. All the others are from the Old Testament.

The wavering yet rock-solid faith Hunter found in the Old Testament sustained him when nothing else could. Even at his most doubt-filled moments, he took comfort in the fact that some of God's favorites had battled the very same demons. He learned that the arms of the Lord are long and wrap around those he loves. I am glad that, in those dark days, Hunter Norwood had the Old Testament to fall back on.

—Philip Yancey

1 min. CLOSING MEDITATION

Let's take a moment to close in prayer.

Dear God, thank you for giving us meaning and purpose, hope and comfort. Sometimes we feel as if you are so far away, yet we know that you are always working out your purposes. Help us to rest in your faithfulness, to keep believing that we matter to you. You love us so much that you sent Jesus to earth at just the right time so that we can receive eternal life through him. We can't imagine how Jesus felt when he took all our sins on himself and was forsaken by you, but we know he did that for us. Thank you for all you have done and are doing in our lives. One day every person and every nation will bow before you, and you will rule in glory in heaven. What a great day that will be! Amen.

—Prayer inspired by Psalm 22:1–5, 22–28